Transforming the IS Organization

ICIT Research Study Team #1
Joyce J. Elam
Michael J. Ginzberg
Peter G. W. Keen
Robert W. Zmud

Contributing Editor
Sharlene Sue Jimenez

International Center for Information Technologies
Washington, D.C.

Published in 1988 by ICIT Press
International Center for Information Technologies
2000 M Street, N.W.
Washington, D.C. 20036

© 1988 by the International Center for Information Technologies.
All rights reserved. No part of this publication may be reproduced, stored in a retrieval system, or transmitted in any form or by any means, electronic, mechanical, photocopy, recording, or otherwise, without the prior written consent of the publisher.

Printed in the United States of America

Library of Congress Cataloging in Publication Data

Transforming the IS organization.

    Includes bibliographies and index.
    1. Information resources management. I. Elam, Joyce J. II. Jimenez, Sharlene Sue. III. ICIT Research Study Team # 1.
T58.64.T73 1988   658.4'038   88-13608
ISBN 0-945098-03-0

Contents

Foreword vii

Preface ix

Background and Overview 1

Chapter One
Roles and Skill Base for the IS Organization 17
Peter G.W. Keen

The Traditional IS Skill Base   18
Roles Versus Tasks   19
Role Analysis   20
Recruiting   25
Lateral Development   32
Education   34
Case Study: Royal Bank of Canada   36
Barriers to Education   38
Summary: Recommendations for Action   39

Chapter Two
**Relationship of Senior Management and the
     IS Organization** 41
Peter G.W. Keen

Authority Versus Responsibility   42
Clarifying the IS Mission   44
Ending the Tradition of Senior
   Management Delegation   48
Ending Organizational Insularity   50
Conclusion: Mutuality   52

Chapter Three
**Building Relationships Throughout the
     Corporate Entity** 55
Robert W. Zmud

TRANSFORMING THE IS ORGANIZATION

Today's Information Services Context 57
Making Partnership Relations Work 62
Structural Mechanisms 67
Management Systems 73
Conclusion 79
Notes 81

Chapter Four
Establishing Cooperative External Relationships 83
Joyce J. Elam

Markets and Hierarchies: A Framework for Viewing
 the IS Organization 85
Cooperative Arrangements 88
Establishing Cooperative Arrangements for Back
 Office and Support Applications 89
Establishing Cooperative Arrangements for
 Strategic Applications 92
Guidelines for Senior IS Executives Pursuing
 Cooperative Arrangements 96
Notes 98

Chapter Five
Managing IS Risk Through Oversight 99
Michael J. Ginzberg

Oversight: The Responsibility 101
Oversight in IS Today 105
Designing an Oversight System for Information Services 107
Mechanisms for Oversight 114
Summary and Agenda for Action 120
Notes 121

Chapter Six
**Questions and Answers About Transforming
 an IS Organization** 123

Index 131

About the Authors 134

List of Exhibits

1-1. Career Map: Summary of Major Roles............................22
1-2. Role Categories and Ratings 23
1-3. Example of a Role Description From a Major Bank..........26
1-4. Role Set for a Leading Bank 27
1-5. Career Time Boundaries 28
1-6. The Recruit's Learning Curve 31
1-7. The Problem of Career Ambiguity 33
1-8. Education Topics for New Roles 35

2-1. Stereotypical Management Roles 42
2-2. Roles in the IS Organization 53
2-3. Relationship Between IS and Business Managers..............53

3-1. "Push-Pull" Dynamics...59
3-2. Middle Management Actions Facilitating IT
   Innovation in the Business Platform 65
3-3. Middle Management Actions Facilitating IT
   Innovation in the Technology Platform.........................66

5-1. Oversight and Control Responsibility for IS
   Activity 105
5-2. Control Exposure of Systems as Ranked by
   IS Managers 106
5-3. Information Services Activities Matrix:
   Representative Oversight Issues 115
5-4. Characteristics of Oversight Mechanisms 117

FOREWORD

If war is too important to be left to the generals, it can also be said that the competitive potential of information technologies is too important to be left to isolated "technical experts" in back office information service (IS) organizations. A new way to organize for success in the Information Age is needed. That's the basic message of this book.

In business, "survival of the fittest" is rapidly becoming "survival of the best informed." Over the next 10 years, a process of natural selection will reward the companies that adapt—and adapt quickly—to the brave new information-driven world.

A variety of information technologies, from personal computing to electronic mail, are becoming commonplace in corporate offices. But to compete effectively in the coming decade, corporate leaders must shift deeply held attitudes and thinking about the role these technologies can and should play in shaping business strategy.

Information technologies demand new organizational thinking because of two realities of the modern age. First, widespread dissemination of information and knowledge among greater numbers of employees is blurring distinctions between levels and functions in the organization. Second, IS has become an integral and essential strategic resource, not just an "expense" or "overhead" item.

Transforming the IS Organization focuses on the organizational roadblocks that prohibit IS organizations from playing a central role in the modern corporation. The IS organization is the new central nervous system of today's large company. The authors here argue that in the accelerating global marketplace, companies that are equipped to act and react in a timely fashion—to seize opportunities and avoid mistakes—will have an IS organization that is fully integrated with every business department and function.

This position, supported by ample research and numerous case studies, makes this ground-breaking book an extremely useful tool for moving IS organizations from the computer room to the board room. The book offers guidelines for ending the traditional insularity of IS and for building partnerships at all levels in the company. It

TRANSFORMING THE IS ORGANIZATION

demonstrates the value of enlarging IS's role in shaping the company's strategic objectives, and describes the importance of cross-training IS personnel to prepare them as strategic role-players.

The mission of the International Center for Information Technologies (ICIT) is to help business leaders plan for, manage, and use information technologies—all of which will prove increasingly indispensable in the coming decade. How to best exploit information technologies must command the urgent attention of top corporate executives seeking competitive advantage in the Information Age.

William G. McGowan
Chairman and Chief Executive Officer
MCI Communications Corporation

PREFACE

This is a time of fundamental change for IS organizations. Users are becoming increasingly sophisticated in applying information technology; information is becoming increasingly important to implementing business strategies; executives are becoming increasingly concerned with ensuring that real value is gained from investments in information technology. More and more of the expenditures for information services and products are outside of the control of the IS organization. There is little disagreement that the IS organization of the 1990s will be radically different from the IS organization of today. The aim of this book is to contribute something distinctive to the ongoing discussion of what these differences will be.

Transforming the IS Organization is based on the results of a research study initiated by ICIT in January 1987. Participating in the research were Peter G.W. Keen, Executive Director of ICIT; Joyce Elam, Harvard Business School; Michael Ginzberg, Case Western Reserve University; and Robert Zmud, Florida State University. Each member of the research study team was responsible for contributing one chapter to this book. The research study manager was Dan Twomey, MCI (then Managing Director of ICIT). Research support was provided by Martha Ruh and Sharlene Sue Jimenez of ICIT. Jimenez was responsible for the introductory and the concluding chapters of this book.

Over a period of several months, the team worked together to shape the research study, share ideas, give progress reports, and review preliminary drafts of papers. In September 1987, the results of their research were presented to an audience of academics, consultants, and IS executives at a conference held in Washington, D.C. The attendees were challenged to evaluate the presentations in small discussion groups and to prepare questions for the research study team. The attendees' enthusiastic response resulted in a question and answer session which appears here as the final chapter.

This book reflects the research study team's view that the IS organization can no longer be the stand-alone organization that it has been in the past. Building partnerships, implementing effective over-

TRANSFORMING THE IS ORGANIZATION

sight procedures, and developing IS professionals with business as well as technical skills are seen as the key to facilitating the integration of the IS organization with the rest of the business. This book is for those who will be leading the transformation of the IS organization. It is hoped that they will find it a useful guide.

Peter G.W. Keen
Executive Director
International Center for Information Technologies

BACKGROUND AND OVERVIEW

Hostility and change have become facts of life in American business: competition is global and increasingly fierce; industry boundaries and the nature of the marketplace seem to change on a daily basis; and Wall Street is involved in a frenzy of takeovers, acquisitions, and mergers. To exist in this environment, business firms increasingly depend on their ability to locate "competitive advantages" that will allow them not only to survive but to grow. Information technology is being recognized as a key means for gaining or maintaining market positions in many business environments.

Competitive opportunities facilitated by information technology cannot be fully exploited unless today's information services (IS) organization significantly changes its mission and management practices. Among staff functions, the IS organization is routinely rated last and criticized as being slow, inefficient, expensive, and unresponsive. The increasing number of non-IS professionals being appointed to direct IS organizations clearly illustrates senior management's lack of confidence in the ability of today's IS organization to change from within.

Transforming an IS organization effectively is not an easy task given historical developments. Throughout the 1960s and 1970s IS organizations were self-contained units with absolute control over information resources and the design and implementation of computer-based systems. The development agenda was straightforward from a business perspective (although IS organizations frequently struggled with the technical complexities), and interactions among the IS organization, senior management, and other business units were minimal, at best. In the mid to late 1970s users showed signs of becoming more technically sophisticated. That, coupled with a rapid drop in the price of information technology, forced IS organizations to relinquish absolute control over information resources and begin determining how they could work with the rest of the organization. From many users' perspective, IS organizations did this poorly, resulting in adversarial rather than productive working relationships.

Many significant changes occurred within IS organizations during the late 1970s and early 1980s. The IS organization was reduced in size and many of its systems development functions were dispersed to user departments, leaving a core of backbone systems in the traditional IS organization. More than 50 percent of total organizational expenditures on information products and services now lie outside the formal IS organization's control. Current trends have IS organizations providing systems and services that business units can provide for themselves only when there are compelling business advantages to do so.

The New Mission

The future of the IS organization is a subject of much speculation. The withering away of the IS organization foreseen by John Dearden of the Harvard Business School needs to be taken seriously.[1] According to Dearden, users will be able to obtain information systems of higher quality and at lower prices from outside companies specializing in software development rather than from the in-house IS organization. In addition to the economic advantages, the decentralization of software development will allow a user to assume full responsibility for judging and assessing the importance and priority of applications. In this way, users can ensure the quality of systems on which their ability to function depends.

If the primary mission of the IS organization revolves around systems development, Dearden's prediction will likely prove correct. Systems development almost certainly will not be a major part of the IS organization of tomorrow's mission. The question then arises as to what activities, if any, will be. John Rockart and Michael Treacy, both of the MIT Sloan School of Management, agree with Dearden that line management will be charged with identifying, prioritizing, and developing application systems.[2] What they see remaining for the IS organization is (a) the management of the hardware and software infrastructure necessary to run the line management applications efficiently and (b) the education of line management in the use of existing and emerging technologies.

We agree that the systems development for user departments will also cease to be the primary mission of new IS organizations. However, our concept of what this primary mission will be is broader than the one proposed by Rockart and Treacy. Facilitating business change will be a key activity in this mission. The IS organization will often act not as the initiator and director of change, but as a multiplier in the change process. For example, when financial managers and professionals lead a radical redesign of cash management policies and procedures, the responsibility of the IS organization is to insure that information requirements are met and that the system implementation is carefully planned and executed.

Of course, sometimes personnel in the business unit most intimately associated with a redesign effort lack the vision to initiate and direct such a change effort. If such a change initiative is both necessary (for business success) and technology-based, the IS organization may need to recognize the change opportunity and carry out the change effort (while not being perceived by the target business unit as usurping its authority). Thus, a key goal in the mission of the IS organization is to position itself so it can serve needed and appropriate roles in business change processes—initiator of change, leader of change, implementor of change, or supporter of change.

Some may think this new role as facilitator of change implies that technology will become a trivial concern of the IS organization. This is not true—technology matters. In fact, it matters more than ever before. The IS organization of tomorrow will be responsible for

1. Providing the technical infrastructure that enables others to specify their own information services;
2. Guaranteeing the integrity of the corporate architecture and providing an integration path for new systems and new technologies;
3. Anticipating when demand for information technology resources will occur so that the IS organization can prepare to meet that need.

In terms of software support, future IS organizations will be responsible for the mega-projects, i.e., those projects that cross organizational boundaries. Mega-projects have strategic implications; they are expensive, and they call for non-commodity services that can only be provided by making the most of expertise within the IS organization. Such systems can be, and usually are, highly technical.

Much of this book will be devoted to further articulating ideas on the new mission of IS organizations. As a starting point, we present below the mission statement of the Royal Bank of Canada to illustrate what we expect the mission of tomorrow's IS organization to include.

The Royal Bank of Canada

Chartered in 1869, the Royal Bank of Canada is that country's largest bank, with assets over $100 billion Canadian. The Bank comprises

TRANSFORMING THE IS ORGANIZATION

more than 1,400 domestic branches and over 150 subsidiaries and affiliates operating in 45 countries, making it one of the largest retail banks in the world and the sixth largest in North America. The information systems organization of the Royal Bank, known as Operations and Systems (O&S), is staffed by over 3,500 personnel, of whom two-thirds are dedicated to operating computer and network facilities and one-third are development staff.

Changes in the IS organization began in 1983 when the manager in charge of O&S retired. The exiting manager's charge had been to control costs to hold down the budget, after what had been years of rapid IS growth. As is often the case, such a narrow mission resulted in limited new development activities and questionable morale. Yet, the Bank's business growth still produced an escalating budget. The newly appointed manager, who had prior IS experience, had headed strategic planning for the previous four years. He had some different ideas of what the IS organization should do. After extensive collaboration with the O&S vice presidents, he generated a series of statements describing what the O&S professional "stands for":

> I stand for:
> - Product management self-sufficiency in managing the application of technology for the creation of products and services, while retaining the economies of productivity gains through using common systems or modules.
> - Clarifying and promulgating technology access rules (policies, standards, and guidelines) in such areas as security, architecture, and network interface which will allow more people to apply technology to their function themselves.
> - Excellence in the design, development, acquisition, integration, and operation of service delivery in support of the sales and services efforts of the bank to its customers.
> - Developing and implementing a "back office" in support of services and services delivery which is better than any other financial institution in Canada and is competitive in the other key markets.
> - A ten-fold increase in services, service delivery and control systems . . . and [consideration of] all forms of design, development, acquisition, integration, operations, and business arrangements or organizations that support this.
> - Being an information services enterprise, aggressively pursuing,

BACKGROUND AND OVERVIEW

developing, and managing new technology-related business for the bank.
- People saying what they will do, doing what they say, and rewarding those who consistently deliver on their promises.
- And above all, I stand for making the Royal Bank a good place to do good business.

These statements represent an attitude and environment that we see as characteristic of future IS organizations. From a business perspective, the O&S organization will become much more a part of the Bank rather than a staff department servicing the various business units. More importantly, the new O&S organization will become a proactive advocate of the increased use of technology throughout the Bank. The Bank's O&S organization now accepts as part of its role the tasks of seeking market niches for business growth and expansion through the use of technology, and developing and managing these technology-based business activities.

Overview

This book presents an agenda for the foundation of any effort to transform an IS organization in order to accomplish its new mission. The key elements of this agenda are

1. Roles and Skill Base for the IS Organization
2. Relationship of Senior Management and the IS Organization
3. Building Relationships Throughout the Corporate Entity
4. Establishing Cooperative External Relationships
5. Managing IS Risk Through Oversight

Each of the elements of this agenda is covered in detail in subsequent chapters. The need and rationale for each is discussed below.

Roles and Skill Base for the IS Organization

A new mission for the IS organization requires a rethinking of the roles and responsibilities of IS professionals. Words such as *innovator*, *marketer*, *consultant*, and *broker* will likely become more associated with IS professionals than words such as *developer*, *maintainer*, and *technocrat*.

TRANSFORMING THE IS ORGANIZATION

It is often facetiously pointed out that the IS organization is composed of technicians and ivory-tower thinkers unaware of the business or the marketplace. Too often, this statement accurately characterizes IS professionals, and, as one moves from one business to another or one industry to another, differences in the skills, attitudes, and loyalties of IS professionals seem to be few.

A primary factor behind this homogeneous view of IS professionals is that for career growth, the professional must have an experience base that is firm-independent but hardware/software-dependent. Look at any recruiting announcement, be it for programmers, analysts or managers. What stands out are a string of mnemonics: CICS, IMS, COBOL, DB/2, MVS, etc. The traditional career path in IS proclaims the system programmers as the "kings and queens." They are the special breed, compared to the business-wise analyst who understands organizational politics and technology. Second in line most often are those involved with the technical side of new system development, followed by those who maintain systems (it is often perceived to be the "kiss of death" to be told you've been assigned to maintenance work). The final group consists of the operations staff.

A good example of how this pattern is beginning to break down can be observed at Morgan Stanley, a global investment banking firm. Morgan Stanley provides a full product line in the financial services industry. The firm began changing the profile of its MIS staff in 1980 through a number of initiatives:

1. Recruitment of top undergraduates representing all majors;
2. Cross-functional career-pathing;
3. An intensive in-house training program, covering both business and technology themes;
4. A compensation program based 100 percent on performance;
5. Emphasis on promoting from within rather than hiring from the outside.

An IS expert at Morgan Stanley believes that the training program in particular is responsible for the exemplary manner in which IS operates. In the first phase, before new recruits become part of the professional staff, they spend 4–9 months gaining proficiency at their first assignment, which typically is installing phones or operating computers. After new recruits complete that first level as trainees, they enter the second phase of the program as professionals. This phase focuses on technical training and ultimately, management training,

BACKGROUND AND OVERVIEW

with appropriate business and finance training occurring as it relates to specific assignments.

The combination of experience in this two-phase program, both hands-on and business-flavored, makes possible the all-important relationship between IS and the users. At Morgan Stanley, this relationship is so highly valued it has become one of the three main tenets of the IS mission statement. Within IS, the user relationship is compared more to that of a customer/supplier. To further enhance the level of utility and quality of interface between IS and the "customers," Systems Development has been structured around the user's business units. The training program, the organizational structure, and the human capital have all been factors contributing to Morgan Stanley's reputation as one of the best on Wall Street.

Managing Information Services: the Politics of Ambiguity

How successful future IS organizations will be in carrying out a new mission will depend on the ability to establish strong working relationships with senior management. This is critical; the IS organization itself cannot make changes necessary to carry out its new mission. It needs the support and help of senior management in several key areas.

First, IS planning must be integrated with business planning. This is particularly important because IS lead time is required. The roadblock to competitive advantage is rarely information technology itself; rather it is the time needed for implementation. It is already too late to affect 1990, but if information technology is to be a strategic part of the business plan of 1992, the IS organization must be included in planning that part now.

The IS organization must also be aware of and involved in the business vision when planning the technical infrastructure or architecture. A firm that wants to use information technology to embark on a new strategic initiative is paralyzed without the proper architecture in place to support the initiative. The architecture must reflect the direction the business will take based on the marketplace. Involving the IS organization in the business vision provides the proper flexibility and support and enables it to plan for the needed architecture.

The IS organization must no longer be considered a pure cost center. Rather, senior management should reorganize the IS organization as a quasi-profit center, with (a) a fixed budget for providing common, critical services such as the technical infrastructure that serves

TRANSFORMING THE IS ORGANIZATION

common, critical services such as the technical infrastructure that serves all users; and (b) a flexible budget for providing products and services that are purchased at the option of the users at prices set by the IS organization. Treating the IS organization as a cost center carries with it a basic assumption that information services are a drain rather than a contributor to corporate profitability. Recasting the IS organization as a quasi-profit center encourages behavior—both by the IS organization and the users of its services—to allocate resources toward those activities that will return the greatest value. Recasting makes it possible for the IS organization to consider whether or not it makes sense to supply certain services itself or let the users purchase the services outside. It also encourages users to make better decisions about how to use and acquire information services.

Finally, investments in information technology and resources are the fastest growing contender for business capital in the 1980s. Senior management and the IS organization need to decide together which investments are critical to the success—and even survival—of the firm. As the use of information technology becomes more tied to the core business, any change in IS has more serious ramifications for the business as a whole than it did in the past. In this light, an uninformed move by the IS organization can be compared to gambling with the business.

Relationship of Senior Management and the IS Organization

Building a strong working relationship between the IS organization and senior management requires some fundamental changes in the ways that the senior IS executive and the business' top management team interact. Some firms noted for their aggressive and effective deployment of information technology already have forged these critical links, thereby allowing the senior IS executive to be accepted as an influential member of the top management's governing body.

There are four potential barriers to forming this relationship between a firm's IS organization and senior management. The first barrier is the bane of any IS manager's existence: the gap between authority and responsibility. This dilemma must be settled at the senior management level, first taking into account the overall mission of the IS organization and then justifying it in business terms. This point relates to the second potential barrier: a general ambiguity about the

BACKGROUND AND OVERVIEW

IS mission and its vision. Involving senior management in articulating an IS vision can clarify the use of information technology as part of a global strategy rather than merely as another expense item.

The third barrier a firm might confront is the temptation of senior management to delegate the duty of directing. This practice is common when senior management lacks either intuition or a fondness for cost-based justifications. However, when a firm deals with any component of its capital commitments that involves such risk, cost, and lead times, delegation simply cannot be a strategy.

The final potential barrier to achieving and maintaining a relationship between the IS organization and senior management is organizational insularity. Within any level or function in the firm, the effects of insularity can be equally disastrous. A senior business manager guilty of insularity is in danger of being overtaken by an unnoticed competitive threat. Insularity within the IS organization can cause it to operate without regard for the firm's needs, processes, and priorities. Raising senior management's level of awareness of this situation, and establishing an active dialogue between IS and senior management must be at the top of the action agenda for all IS managers.

The Sara Lee Company provides an excellent practical example of the relationship between senior management and IS. A process of change began with a reassessment of senior management's IS strategies. In order to continue to grow and prosper as a business, the company needed to change the way its information resources were used in both an organizational and strategic sense. Sara Lee senior management produced many guidelines to enable these changes. However, the single directive that catalyzed the transition in the IS organization was an increased emphasis on the relationship between IS and senior management. Some specific goals that the company set out to meet included:

- Provide leadership in the development of information systems management personnel;
- Improve the awareness and involvement of senior management in IS planning;
- Involve the total organization in setting IS strategy.

To meet these goals and others, Sara Lee began a vast education program aimed at both IS managers and senior management. This program, along with special workshops held by consultants, helped to forge a relationship between IS and senior management. These efforts enabled IS and senior managers throughout the business to communicate with a common vocabulary and a shared understanding of the strategic importance of IS. Sara Lee realized nearly immediate benefits from these activities to bring IS and senior management together. A major one was the implementation of a nationwide state-of-the-art information system that completely restructured the firm's distribution operations. The subsequent increases in productivity and the decreases in cost and inventory were directly attributable to the installation of this system. Through the senior management and IS partnership, this plan not only came to fruition, it produced positive results.

Building Relationships Throughout the Corporate Entity

The new IS mission demands that new relationships be established between corporate and divisional IS groups and managers/users throughout the organization. For this to occur, the hostile and mistrustful view of IS professionals often held by other organizational members must be overcome. The first step lies with IS professionals facing up to the fact that, in business terms, they really haven't delivered.

Today's innovative IS products and services have the potential to bring the back office and the front office together. When this occurs, stress often intensifies and political issues surface. This environment can be detrimental to working relationships among individuals brought together to initiate and implement business changes. In order to establish and nurture effective working relationships among these individuals, management must provide structural mechanisms to instill mutual respect, trust, and properly focused motivation and commitment. Implementing such mechanisms is another crucial agenda item.

An example of such a relationship can be seen in the Royal Bank of Canada's efforts to develop a Letter of Credit (LC) product. In the mid 1980s, as deregulation of the Canadian financial industry loomed, the Royal Bank found that a competitor from outside Canada was introducing an LC product to a few of its clients. To respond to this threat, the Royal Bank broke down all traditional barriers by establishing a software development team consisting of individuals from Operation and Systems, Marketing, *and* the clients themselves.

The idea was to rapidly prototype a PC-based LC product and to test that prototype with a few selected clients. The marketing group worked closely with the systems group and this team took the product

BACKGROUND AND OVERVIEW

produced the product under schedule and met the challenge of the external threat.

Part of the process necessary to establish this working relationship was to redefine the boundaries between the working groups making up the team. This meant flattening the organizational structure by three levels and allowing individuals across groups to have access to each other's resources. It also meant going against the organizational grain in some instances. But, as one individual in the LC project stated, "We were the project, and we saw no formal boundaries among our groups."

Establishing Cooperative External Relationships

In an environment where no single vendor holds an exclusive position regarding any information technology (for example, one doesn't automatically go to AT&T for telephones or to IBM for computers), new relationships are required between the IS organization and all of its vendors. In addition, the dynamic changes in the nature of markets (such as those associated with point-of-sale devices in retailing and financial services and electronic data interchange techniques in manufacturing and wholesaling) and the huge investments associated with initiating or reacting to these changes provide the opportunity, or necessity, to form new types of cooperative arrangements that extend beyond organizational boundaries.

As technology-based cooperative arrangements propel the IS organization into the middle of a firm's strategy setting and implementing processes, new skill-sets and relationships must be acquired. Such activities can be new and threatening to many IS personnel. Likewise, line managers responsible for these strategic thrusts suddenly find themselves dependent on IS personnel in critical business matters, also likely a new and threatening experience. Devising effective means of forming and managing relationships with external parties thus becomes another key action item.

A preview to the types of cooperative arrangements that one will find in the IS organization of tomorrow is the $200 million application development project between Ford and IBM to develop integrated office systems. A team of 50 Ford and IBM executives is designing the system to fit Ford's needs and is jointly overseeing installation. In establishing this cooperative arrangement, IBM was forced to abandon its sales approach of the past decade. "They asked us to start with a blank piece of paper and redefine how the relationship between the two companies should work" says one IBM assistant group executive, " so we did." As a part of this new relationship, IBM is lifting its usual shroud of secrecy about future products. The confidential information provided to Ford by IBM allows Ford to take advantage of any planned but unannounced products in designing its new office systems.[3]

Managing IS Risk Through Oversight

The final element of the agenda touches on all of the others: the need for oversight in managing risk in the IS organization. Two key factors combine to increase the risks and consequences associated with the IS organization. First, IS activities are increasingly complex, expensive, and widespread. Second, IS personnel are routinely distributed among a central IS department, divisional IS departments, and functional IS departments. Often in this environment, no single individual is positioned to monitor and manage risk. Ultimately, the CEO has the overall responsibility and authority to monitor and control. However, in an operational, detail sense, it is often unclear who is responsible and whether authority and responsibility are aligned.

No one individual can possibly provide the oversight necessary to manage a devolved IS environment, so the oversight responsibility must rest with senior management while the execution of this responsibility must be distributed. Within this framework, the IS organization must be responsible for assuring that there is an effective system for IS planning, policy-setting, and control. This includes the role of designing a planning system and assigning control responsibilities. The responsibility for executing these controls generally is distributed among the users of IS and the IS manager.

Related Research

The amorphous nature of the future of IS organizations coupled with obvious importance has served to raise the industry's level of interest on this topic. Through books such as this, practitioners and researchers alike are continually contributing to a growing body of knowledge. The themes and ideas presented here relate to work completed by other experts in this field.

A recurring theme in this book and in most of the industry literature

BACKGROUND AND OVERVIEW

is how the responsibilities for delivering information services should be distributed throughout an organization. The way in which one of the largest banks in the United States, Manufacturers Hanover Trust, addressed this question is described in a recent article by H. Edward Nyce, head of Manufacturers Hanover Information Technologies Services, and Antoinette La Belle, Vice President in charge of organizational planning.[4]

Manufacturers Hanover Trust recently underwent a major reorganization in which five strategic sectors were formed, each having profit and loss responsibility. The challenge facing Nyce was to determine how nine major functions (Strategic Planning and Control, Marketplace Intelligence and Technology Research, Architecture Planning, Resource Planning and Acquisition, Systems Development, Computer and Telecommunications Operations, Policy and Standards Management, Human Resources Management, and Risk Management) should be distributed between the corporate group and its five strategic sectors. The solution divided responsibilities for activities within these nine major functions between the corporate group and the sectors. It also defined the critical equilibrium point for the organization.

We agree that centralization/decentralization is not the issue. The solution to the most effective delivery of information services will fall between the absolute extremes of decentralization and centralization. By focusing on the relationships between IS and the rest of the organization, we address a critical role for the IS organization of tomorrow regardless of where the organization comes out on the centralization/decentralization continuum.

Another theme repeated throughout the chapters of this book, especially in Chapter 2, is the importance of senior management and the IS organization sharing a vision of how information technology can be used within the organization. The presence or absence of this high-level vision can be critical in a company's bid to use its information resources strategically. This line of thought is echoed in a study by Zmud, Boynton, and Jacobs[5] which found that a clear vision of information technology in relation to its present and future impact on the company must be articulated by the senior management. It is necessary, however, for the IS organization to play a critical role in this process of educating senior management on the value and potential of IS. It follows that the IS manager must be a participant in the company's strategy formulation.

Other studies have described the new roles and skills that will be

13

required of IS professionals as we look ahead.[6,7,8] All of the studies point out that IS managers need to recognize that their role is changing from that of a person with absolute control over information processing to one who consults with, educates, and trains users. A forthcoming article by Ginzberg and Baroudi points out the lack of adequate knowledge concerning IS professionals' careers and how to manage them.[9] Chapter 1 by Peter Keen examines this issue in more detail, focusing on the nature of the traditional skill base, recruiting, role vs. skill, education, and lateral development. Robert Zmud, in Chapter 3, expands on this theme by explaining the importance of the career path. Essentially, in order to become the hybrid technical-business managers necessary for the transformation of successful IS organizations, managers and professionals in the IS organization need to move through a succession of job assignments within both the line and IS organizations.

Summary

The goal of this book is to give you some insight on the shape of things to come. Certainly some elements of future IS organizations cannot be predicted now. However, we have tried to limit the impact of the unknowns, and in so doing, provide both senior management and the leadership of the IS organizations of today with some guidelines for transformation.

Notes

1. Dearden, John. "The Withering Away of the IS Department," *Sloan Management Review*, Summer 1987, pp. 87–91.
2. Buday, R. "MIT Professor: MIS Future Lies in Technology, Not Strategy," *Information Week*, June 23, 1986, p. 32.
3. Hampton, William. "How IBM Wooed Ford Into a More Meaningful Relationship," *Business Week*, March 30, 1987, p. 87.
4. La Belle, Antoinette, and H. Edward Nyce. "Whither the IT Organization?," *Sloan Management Review*, Summer 1987, pp. 75–85.
5. Zmud, Robert W., Andrew C. Boynton, and Gerry C. Jacobs. "The In-

formation Economy: A New Perspective for Effective Information Systems Management," *Data Base*, Fall 1986, pp. 17–23.
6. Benjamin, Robert J., Charles Dickinson, Jr., John F. Rockart. "Changing the Role of the Corporate Information Systems Officer," *MIS Quarterly*, September 1985, pp. 177–188.
7. Lucas, Henry C. "Utilizing Information Technology: Guidelines for Managers," *Sloan Management Review*, Fall 1986, pp. 39–47.
8. Rockart, John F., Leslie Ball, and Christine V. Bullen. "The Future Role of the Information Systems Executive," *MIS Quarterly*, Special Issue 1982, pp. 1–14.
9. Ginzberg, Michael J., and J.J. Baroudi. "MIS Careers—A Theoretical Perspective," CACM, June 1988.

CHAPTER ONE

ROLES AND SKILL BASE FOR THE IS ORGANIZATION
PETER G.W. KEEN

In the world of information systems, machinery is well cared for. Machines have maintenance budgets, vendors offer an array of diagnostic and testing equipment, and mainframes are enshrined in perfect, dustless working environments. However, technical professionals are not nearly so well treated. They are a valuable capital resource that needs to be maintained to avoid depreciation. For the next decade, the main management problems concerning telecommunications and computers will center around people, not technology. Senior management vision, policy, and education are critical resources as firms face three major interdependent challenges:

1. To build a new level of management awareness so that business executives lead, not delegate, the development of information technologies (IT);
2. To mobilize the entire organization for an era of radical change in work, structure, and business practices created via IT;
3. To reposition the information services function to handle a far broader range of roles, responsibilities, relationships, and skills.

This chapter focuses on the third issue: building the skill base needed to reposition the IS organization. The discussion provides these specific recommendations for action:

1. Bring together the generally disparate units handling systems development and voice and data communications.
2. Identify the critical roles IS must fill to meet its mission over the next 3–7 years.

TRANSFORMING THE IS ORGANIZATION

3. Define the new career trajectories and provide needed lateral development, education, and reeducation.
4. Reevaluate recruiting options and recruiters.

The Traditional IS Skill Base

In most organizations, information services (data processing, information systems, etc.) have been built around the traditional core of technical work: designing, developing and running large application systems. The mainstream career path has been from computer programmer or systems analyst to project leader to manager. Clear differences in relative status within IS can be observed:

- System programmers have for a long time been the technical elite because of their knowledge of the most complex aspect of business computing: mainframe operating systems.
- Application development has been the central activity in terms of both career opportunities and how work is organized and managed.
- Operations definitely has been lower status.

Information systems and telecommunications organizations have developed along very separate paths. Telecommunications has largely been built around voice services and operations, with relatively little overlap of skills with IS, even though more and more aspects of computing are interdependent with telecommunications. As a result, in many—perhaps even most—organizations, IS professionals know relatively little about voice communications, most voice specialists are unfamiliar with data communications, and many telecommunications experts do not understand high-volume, large-scale transaction processing.

This is a recipe for disaster. The entire direction of IT is towards integration of computing and communications. Thus it is vital that voice and data communications and information systems be brought under the same organizational umbrella, so that an information services organization can be positioned to provide integrated thinking about increasingly integrated technology.

Just bringing computing and communications together is easy to accomplish. The difficulty is that the traditional skill base and corresponding career structure of information services are too narrow and inflexible to meet new demands.

- System programmers represent only one part of a technical service unit that covers a bewildering range of technologies, with little experience and rapid change.
- Application development is no longer the dominating aspect of IS work. End user computing, office technology, personal computers, packaged systems, distributed processing, electronic publishing, and the like are transforming the role of IS from building systems to supporting product and service innovation.
- Maintenance, far from being lower in status than development, often requires the very best technical talent. In an era of on-line customer service and electronic support for more and more aspects of business, the quality of operations, reliability, service, and efficiency depend increasingly on old computer systems that were never designed to handle today's volumes and demands for fast, reliable service. "Maintenance" is really management of a critical business capital asset.
- Similarly, Operations have become a strategic skill area. When a bank's ATM network or an airline's reservation system is down, so is its business. The complexity of such systems makes diagnosis, trouble-shooting, and emergency action new elements in business planning and decision-making; the result is the need for new skills.

Roles Versus Tasks

Building a skill base begins by defining the roles IS must fill. On the whole, IS professionals' work and career development have been based on tasks rather than on roles. The difference is important for IS. Tasks relate to what people do and the content knowledge they need; roles relate to how they operate. The task of traditional systems development mainly required knowledge of COBOL, particular hardware, and operating systems environments and techniques for design, coding, and testing. Technical experience was the main criterion for career growth.

Now, many types of systems development require a far broader set of attitudes, skills, and processes.

- Close interaction at all stages of development with nontechnical users;
- Business and functional knowledge;
- Understanding of nontechnical aspects of the context of the system: work, workers and working, ergonomics, organizational procedures, etc.;

TRANSFORMING THE IS ORGANIZATION

- The ability to communicate and listen well, and to act as an educator and a consultant.

The role of development support is broader than the task of applications development.

For many IS professionals, these new requirements create ambiguity and stress. In particular, the more senior ones have spent up to 20 years learning their craft, only to hear that the rules are being changed. How do they adapt? How does management help them do so? Almost all of their training continues to focus on tasks and technology. Whenever the technology changes or a major new vendor product is launched, they are given a course or a manual. Job ads provide a checklist of the desired task skills: "At least five years experience with CICS, MVS, COBOL. Knowledge of DB2 and C desirable." On the nontechnical components of their new or emerging roles, help is harder to come by.

One consequence of the needed shift from tasks to roles is that the word *user* is an inappropriate term to describe colleagues and clients with whom IS must work cooperatively and coresponsibly. Users are an abstraction. Rather than dealing with a single entity IS has a contractual responsibility to clients and an organizational one to colleagues. It can keep users at a distance. The new roles, mission, and responsibility of IS mean that the word *partner* must be substituted for *user*. Partnership involves informed, trusting, credible equals.

Role Analysis

The new IS skill base has to be defined in terms of roles, not technical tasks: What is the mix of skills and experience we need to operate effectively to support the business, to build a real dialogue with our colleagues and clients, to maintain technical excellence, and to provide first-rate operations and service?

It is obvious that technical experience is just one requirement in IS work. The experience is essential in such areas as operations, maintenance, and large-scale applications, but it is almost irrelevant in other areas where technical currency is key, for example, many aspects of database management, digital communications, and optical storage. In telecommunications, the technical experience of senior staff often shifts from being an asset to a liability; the knowledge base mainly relates to voice communications in a regulated environment when

ROLES AND SKILL BASE FOR THE IS ORGANIZATION

what is needed now is the ability to manage digital communications and to integrate with computing in a multi-vendor context. All of this occurs in a period of massive technical uncertainty; their roles, not just their tasks, have changed.

All existing and emerging IS roles have two main dimensions, each of which has two subcategories (see Exhibit 1-1):

1. Technical
   (a) Breadth of technical experience
   (b) Currency of technical specialty
2. Business/Organizational
   (a) Business and functional knowledge
   (b) Organizational skills

A simple and reliable base for assessing the balance among the four very different skills needed in a particular role is to rate the demand on a scale of 0–5, where:

0 = Irrelevant; no need for this skill
1 = Of very minor importance; a small degree of exposure and experience helpful but not required
2 = Of minor importance
3 = Basic competence/qualification needed
4 = High level of capability required
5 = Absolutely essential; a critical requirement

Roles can then be classified by generating two totals—one for the technical subcategories and one for the business/organizational ones. Hypothetical ratings are shown in Exhibit 1-2 for four very different—and important—IS roles.

The four resulting role categories are defined on the following basis:

1. *Development Support*: Here, the technical components of the role are rated higher than the business and organizational, but the latter are of more than minor importance (i.e., the score is greater than or equal to 5). Traditional applications development puts little if any weight on nontechnical skills and much of the career ambiguity IS professionals now face comes from the demonstrated need for knowledge of the business and organization. It can be very hard for experienced systems development staff to acquire this kind of knowledge late in their careers. They have the skills for the old tasks but not for the new roles.
2. *Business Support*: Many of the new IS roles require strong business

Exhibit 1-1. Career Map: Summary of Major Roles

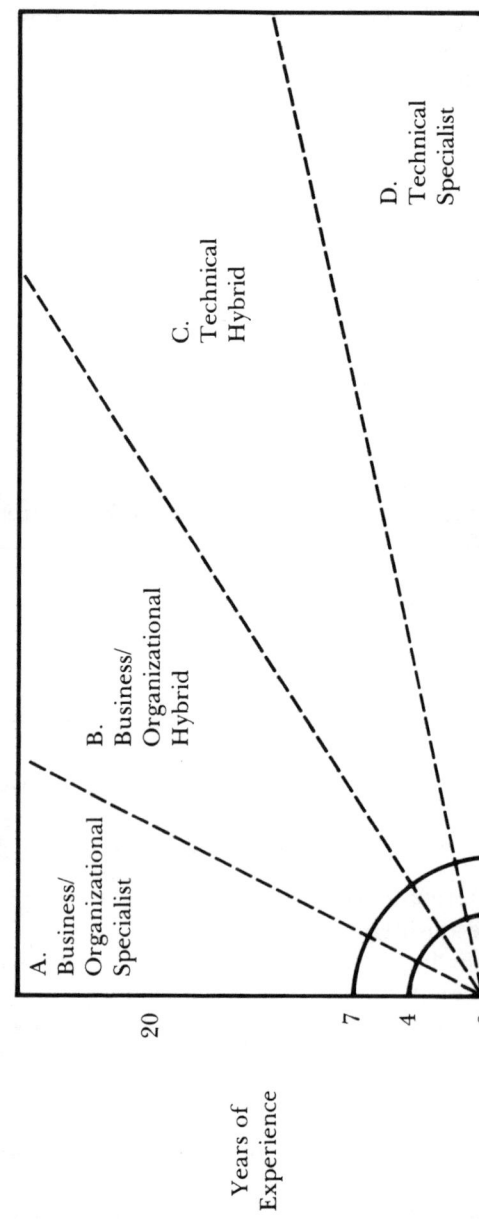

Take difference between technical breadth and currency rating and business and organizational rating

A. Business/Organizational
Difference is negative, with technical breadth and experience less than 5.

B. Business/Organizational Hybrid
Difference is negative, technical sum greater than 5.

C. Technical Hybrid
Difference is positive, business sum is greater than 5.

D. Technical
Difference is positive, business sum is less than 5.

ROLES AND SKILL BASE FOR THE IS ORGANIZATION

Exhibit 1-2. Role Categories and Ratings

	Demand Rating by Role			
Skill/Experience	Data Communications Technical Support	Office Technology Analyst	Application Development Programming	Business Unit IS Planning
1. Technical (T)				
(a) Breadth of experience	3	2	4	2
(b) Currency of specialization	5	3	4	2
Total:	8	5	8	4
2. Business/ Organizational (B/O)				
(a) Business/ functional knowledge	3	4	3	5
(b) Organizational skills	1	5	2	5
Total:	4	9	5	10
Role category:	Development Support	Business Support	Technical Services	Business Services

and organizational expertise and only limited technical skills. In many instances, breadth of experience is either not obtainable because the technology or application is so new, or not valuable because the pace of change makes it obsolescent. Both technical experience and specialization are less important than their business and organization counterparts in many areas of support to end-user computing, office technology, and business product and service development.

Business support roles are ones where there is a need for business fluency and technical literacy—this is indicated by the "B/O" score being greater than that for "T," which in turn is five or greater.

3. *Technical Services*: Here the score for the two technical aspects of IS work are greater than for the business/organizational ones, which

23

TRANSFORMING THE IS ORGANIZATION

add up to less than 5. This means that the business/organizational ratings averaged out to "of minor importance." The example shown above was for data communications technical support. There, currency of specialized knowledge is vital, with reasonable breadth of experience. Organizational skills, communication, the ability to act as a translator between the worlds of business and technology, understanding of work and workers, etc. are entirely subordinate to technical excellence.

4. *Business Services*: The fourth role category requires only limited technical capability and mainly relates to such areas as setting priorities for business unit IS planning, customer service, financial analysis, etc.

Baseline Analysis of Roles

The role categories in Exhibit 1-2 summarize some important implicit messages for IS professionals:

- The main career directions are towards Development Support and Business Support, in client service, through the equivalent of account management, and in project coordination.
- For people whose training and experience have taken them along a largely technical path, it is very hard to move across categories; many project leaders are being pushed towards Business Support and lack adequate people management skills and knowledge of business essentials.
- We no longer have room for average technicians; IS people either have to build business and organizational skills or make sure they maintain technical currency.
- There are no career "paths" now, only career trajectories.
- We are changing the rules on IS people.
  — Experience may no longer be an asset.
  — Old skills are not as valued as before.
  — Seniority does not mean qualification.
  — The hybrid roles that involve a mix of technical and business/organizational skills create career ambiguity; there are no precedents, measurement of performance is hard, and IS professionals run the risk of losing their technical edge while not becoming "real" business people.

The starting point for repositioning IS is to develop a set of appro-

ROLES AND SKILL BASE FOR THE IS ORGANIZATION

priately defined roles. "Appropriate" relates to a firm's business plans and the mission for IS within those plans over the next 3–5 years, defined in terms of priorities, service, and relationships with IS's clients. The specific basis for identifying new roles and redefining old ones is the IS strategic development portfolio: the planned major development projects in the IS capital budget.

This baseline analysis does not take more than a few weeks to develop; the goal is to identify roles, not write detailed job descriptions. Exhibit 1-3 gives an example of a role description developed in a major bank, and Exhibit 1-4 lists the main roles the bank identified; over half of these are new.

The framework shown in Exhibit 1-3 includes assessment of recruiting sources, type of contract, and education and personal development priorities. Each of these is an important element in moving from the baseline analysis of roles to human resource planning; the baseline often reveals the gap between available skills and needed ones. The issue then is how to close it. Management can take action in three main areas:

- Recruiting policy and choice of recruiter;
- Lateral development and movement in and out of IS from and to business units;
- Education and personal development.

Recruiting

Good development staff and technical specialists have always been in short supply. To a large extent, that problem has been compounded by the emphasis placed on technical "aptitude" and on experience. Firms have tended to recruit graduates with technical degrees and to head-hunt for people already in the IS field. Firms that invested heavily in entry-level training often found that they were creating a pipeline into other companies that would pay a premium for the people initially trained elsewhere.

It is surely time to rethink recruiting. The old assumption was that the technology was hard to learn and, by implication, the business was easier to learn. It is no exaggeration to say that any person with strong analytic ability (which is needed to manage the constant process of learning and personal development that marks the shifting IS roles,

Exhibit 1-3. Example of a Role Description From a Major Bank

Role Category: Development Support
Role: Systems Asset Management

Description
This very new role has to be carefully positioned and explained. It changes the status of "maintenance" from the bottom of the ladder to an elite position. The role of a systems asset manager is to take responsibility for a key operational system and to make sure that it is economically effective and efficient. This means trouble-shooting, restructuring bad design, cleaning up code, assessing opportunities to improve technical performance and operational efficiency, etc.

Level in the Organization
Relatively senior. Generally at the level of project manager. In a few instances, the person in this role is the equivalent of the megaproject manager (systems reinvestment for DDA and VISA processing might be future instances). The most technical of the development support roles.

Importance to the Bank's Competitive Plans
Vital. The investment in old systems that were not designed to handle today's volumes and that are poorly documented and structured is immense. Many of these are basic to customer service (ATM code is an obvious instance). Maintenance and operations costs for such systems are growing in absolute and relative terms. They have to be managed as an economic asset with the best development staff assigned as a privilege and career opportunity, not as a perceived punishment.

Recruiting Source
From within Development Support and on occasions Technical Services.

Background and Skills Needed
Experience with the system or group of systems is essential. Needs solid development skills and experience. Needs fairly good business knowledge about the context of the relevant systems and ability to work well with user department staff.

Type of Contract
Mainstream of IS. Generally, taking on this role means that the person intends to move up through Development Support or into Technical Services roles and not into Business Support.

Education and Personal Development Priorities
Structured methods, systems redesign, and reinvestment tools.

Career Quadrant
Estimate of Skill Needs (0–5)

Broad Technical Experience	4
Currency in Technical Specialization	4
Business/Functional Knowledge	3
Organizational/Personal Skills	3

ROLES AND SKILL BASE FOR THE IS ORGANIZATION

Exhibit 1-4. Role Set for a Leading Bank

1. Business Services
- Business measurement and performance analysis
- Capacity anticipation
- Business unit planning support
- Economic planning: Funding, costing and pricing analysis
- High-payoff opportunity analysis
- Corporate information architecture
- Vendor relationship management
- Human asset planning
- Work environment planning

2. Business Support
- Systems account management
- Customer marketing and service support
- Education and training support
- Computer-related risk assessment
- Business systems standards and policies support
- Information library coordination

3. Development Support
- Megaproject coordination
- Project leadership
- Development support
- Systems asset management
- Quality assurance

4. Technical Services
- Architecture and integration planning
- Computing utility specialist services
- Computing utility operations services
- Specialist technical support
- Technology scanning and evaluation

---

technology, applications, and business demands) is now useful to and usable in IS.

The liberal arts major who can easily handle the unstructured nature of support of office technology, the accountant who can develop pricing strategies, or the financial staff analyst who can help end users develop their own systems on personal computers, can easily learn enough about the relevant technology to be effective. They will rarely be able or want to become Development Support specialists working on large scale COBOL projects or designing complex databases, but they are far more likely to feel comfortable in their support and service

TRANSFORMING THE IS ORGANIZATION

role than a traditional applications programmer who has been pushed into it—and out of his or her chosen career niche.

Exhibit 1-5 augments Exhibit 1-3. It shows two career time boundaries, one at roughly 4 years and one at 7. In their first four years, IS recruits have plenty of opportunity to find their niche and to explore the variety of role categories, with very little career risk. They are unlikely to become square pegs in round holes because every skill can be usefully employed.

In the 4–7 year range, professionals need to learn their craft and sharpen their sense of career direction. Very roughly, the development priorities are

- *Business Services*: a solid grounding in business planning, knowledge of a functional area, and exposure to business units at a fairly senior level.

Exhibit 1-5. Career Time Boundaries

[Diagram: A quarter-circle graph with "Years of Experience" on the vertical axis marked 0, 4, 7, 20. Radial sectors labeled "Business Services Roles", "Business Support Roles", "Development Support Roles" (with note: Shift in role demands for IS Managers), and "Technical Services Roles" (with note: Career path of most IS Project Leaders).]

| In the 0-4 year range, individual has plenty of room to explore career trajectories. | In the 4-7 year range, individual needs to build on basic skills and grow into role category. | After 7-10 years, it is extremely hard to move across role categories. |

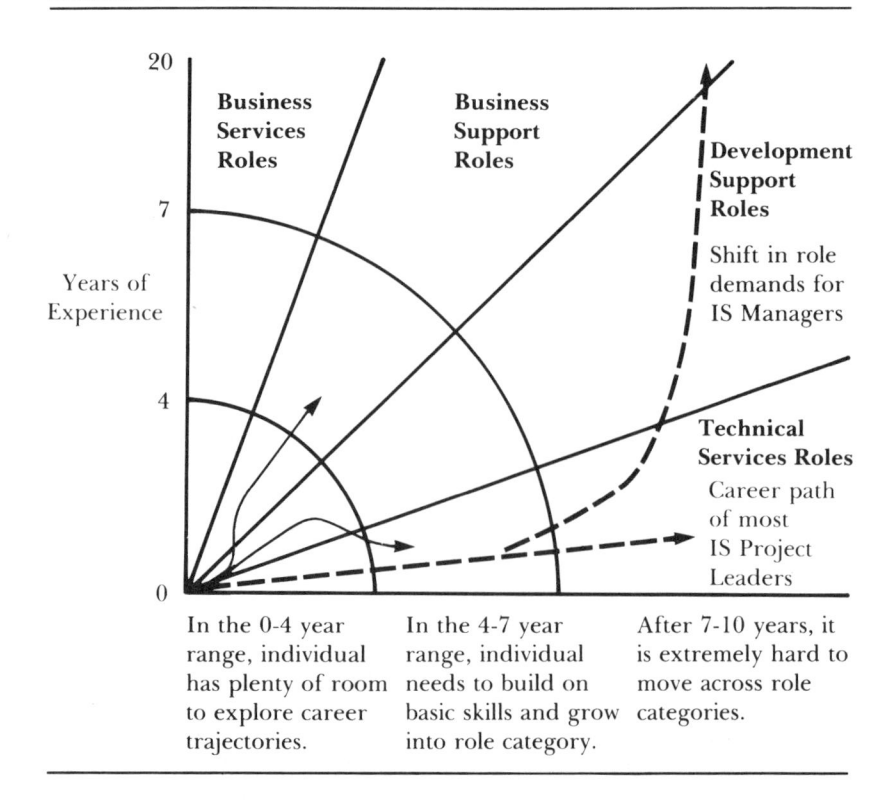

ROLES AND SKILL BASE FOR THE IS ORGANIZATION

- *Business Support*: exposure to the business at a nuts-and-bolts level, development of organizational skills, and close working relationships with the client and colleague community.
- *Development Support*: experience in large-scale projects, education and experience with software productivity methods, development aids, and project management methods (especially user-led ones).
- *Technical Services*: continued in-depth education in a chosen field of expertise and membership in professional societies.

If people can grow into their roles over a four-year period, it is no longer essential that they fit the traditional profile when they are recruited at the entry level. Of course, a computer science graduate is more likely to want to move along a Technical Services career trajectory, but the opportunity is there to shift towards Development Support and Business Support. Similarly, the senior secretary assigned to IS to help train office staff in word processing may well build a much broader knowledge of office technology: electronic publishing, optical storage, document interchange, intelligent optical character reader (OCR), etc.

This argument challenges the established belief that computer people are somehow "different" from others and that technical aptitude is a basic requirement for entry to the field. Obviously, most aspects of Technical Services do involve unusual and idiosyncratic skills. Data modeling, network design, and programming at the "hacker" level are just a few examples. The new importance of the two Support roles must not divert attention from the equal importance of first-rate technical talent in an environment where the business is on-line; technical risk is now business risk and the quality of customer service is a function of the quality of the computer and communications operations.

That said, broadening the recruiting sources is the only way both to locate good people in a market of scarcity of qualified staff in traditional tasks, and to bring in the new attitudes, knowledge, and aptitude required for the hybrid support roles. There is plenty of evidence, albeit fragmented and anecdotal, that this approach works. For example:

- One of the top five computer manufacturers successfully implemented a program of internal recruitment. It selected a small group of secretaries, junior clerical workers, and others who were "non-exempt" personnel, hourly-wage earners with no degrees or profes-

sional qualifications. They were moved through a 20-week training program that taught them the best of structured analysis and design techniques. They were then moved into IS, where a review two years later showed they were rated significantly above average in their performance. The firm has since repeated the program several times, with the same impact.
- The petrochemical industry has generally been a leader in IS organizational developments and in the application of effective development tools, like Exxon's SADT (Structured Analysis and Design Technique). Several firms have moved away from their earlier recruiting of computer science graduates into Technical Service roles because of the vital need for infusion of business attitudes.
- Many banks now have a strong cadre of Development Support Specialists with strong technical expertise in data management and in advanced personal computing (mainframe-micro links, specialist development languages like C, and local area networks rather than just spreadsheets). These people have never been in IS and have no formal technical training. They are finance or accounting staff, largely self-directed, who have shaped a new Business and Development Support role.

Many firms are also recognizing that knowledge of the organization and credibility with users is a primary requirement in many Support roles; thus the best source of recruitment into IS is from elsewhere in the company.

Technical currency and experience is largely organization-independent. A systems programmer is probably close to being fully effective when joining the firm; his or her knowledge of IBM mainframe operating systems translates directly to the new context. It takes at least two years, and probably closer to four, to build organization-dependent experience. Exhibit 1-6 shows the relative impact of the difference in terms of both the productivity of recruits and the cost of losing existing staff; the salary for the systems programmer is higher than for the office technology support role, but the true cost of growing and of having to replace the latter is far higher because of the hidden cost of building organizational experience (the figures shown are only hypothetical, but reasonable).

Clearly, IS units can and should recruit aggressively from inside the organization. They will still need to bring in people from outside, of course, especially for Technical Services and many Development Support roles, where technical aptitude or experience are at a pre-

Exhibit 1-6. The Recruit's Learning Curve

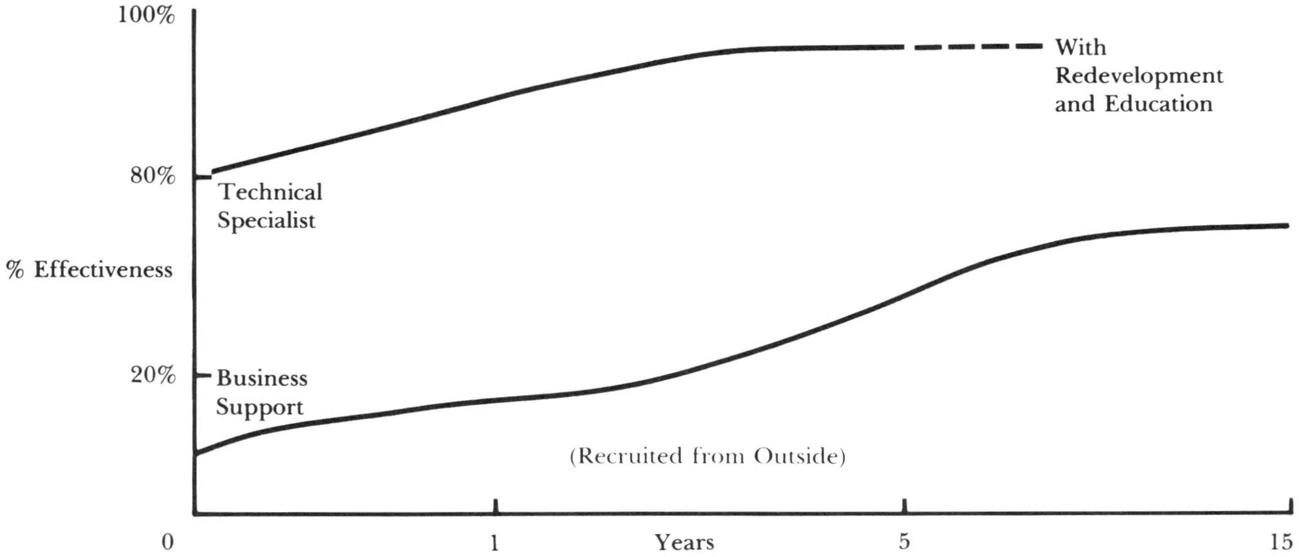

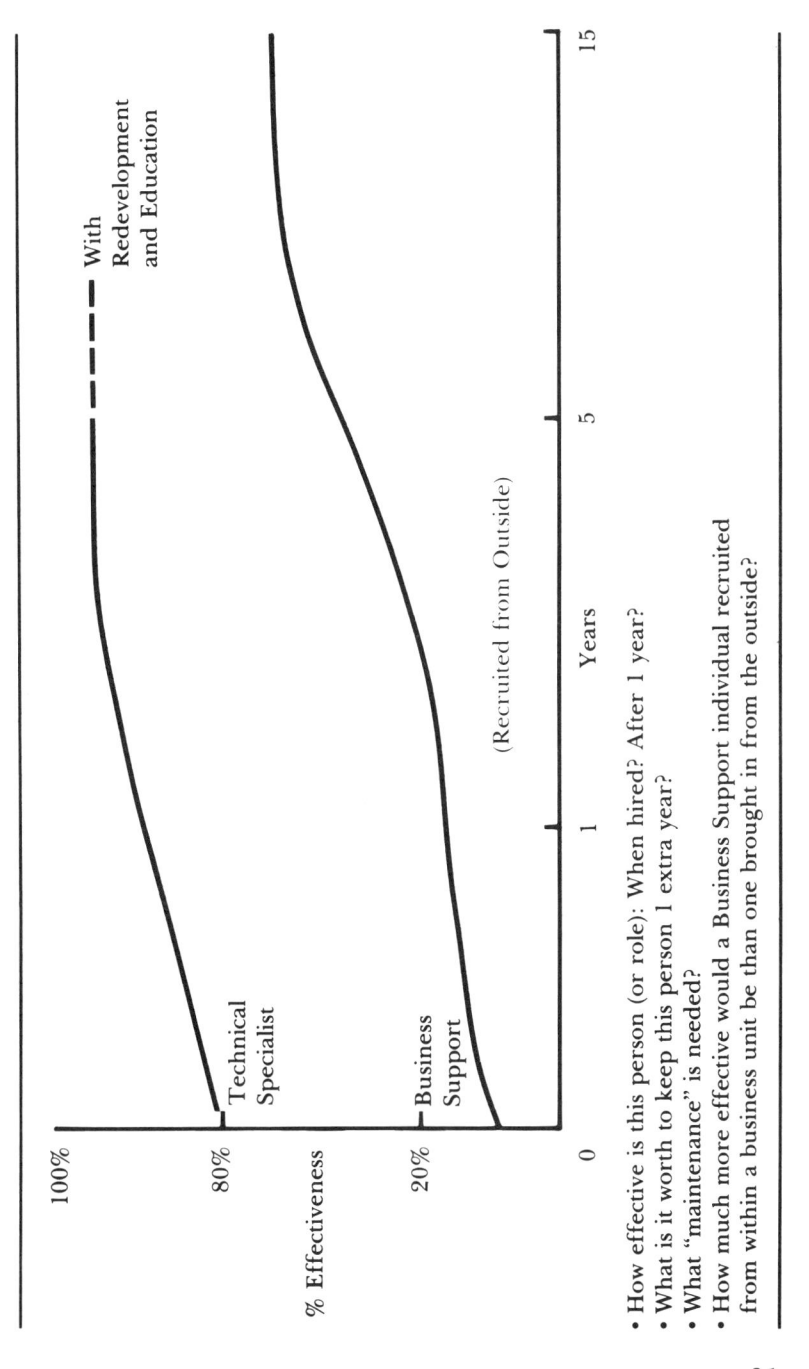

100%
80%
% Effectiveness
20%
Technical Specialist
Business Support
With Redevelopment and Education
(Recruited from Outside)
0
1
Years
5
15

- How effective is this person (or role): When hired? After 1 year?
- What is it worth to keep this person 1 extra year?
- What "maintenance" is needed?
- How much more effective would a Business Support individual recruited from within a business unit be than one brought in from the outside?

TRANSFORMING THE IS ORGANIZATION

mium. If the recommendation made earlier (to recruit business-oriented liberal arts majors) is accepted, they will place a special emphasis on bringing into Business Support, at the entry-level, people with business, not technical, training.

All this makes the IS recruiter an important element in recruiting. In general, the middle- to senior-level IS manager and project leaders who first meet with potential recruits, come out of the old career tradition. Too many of these veterans are not natural managers, are not sensitive to nontechnical issues, or, in some cases, do not recognize the need for people management skills. They naturally tend to recruit in their own image and attract recruits who are on their wavelength. With the best will in the world, the old guard of IS can substantially block any change in the IS culture. In the long run it may be more effective to have users play an active role in recruiting Business Support staff.

Lateral Development

Just as recruiting from within the organization makes it possible to build technical ability on business and organizational skills, moving IS personnel out into partner areas for a six-month to two-year period builds support skills on technical ones. Responsive organizations have increasingly moved their best people out, but have not gotten them back. They are a net exporter of talent.

Senior management can bring this two-way flow in and out of IS into balance and can speed up the cross-fertilization of IS and business people. Movement into and out of IS has to be seen as career enhancement, not some form of punishment.

Exhibit 1-7 illustrates the problem of career ambiguity. "Fast-track" managers or outstanding supervisors who are pulled off their mainstream business trajectory to work on assignment to IS are likely to see themselves falling behind their peers. They are neither becoming IS professionals nor accepted by IS professionals. Similarly, an applications programmer with a solid technical resume will feel that he or she is less marketable or promotable by being moved into the area of "amateur" computing.

Senior management has to establish that information technologies are now so central to the firm that a subset of the future management cadre will be routinely given the lateral development that creates

ROLES AND SKILL BASE FOR THE IS ORGANIZATION

Exhibit 1-7. The Problem of Career Ambiguity

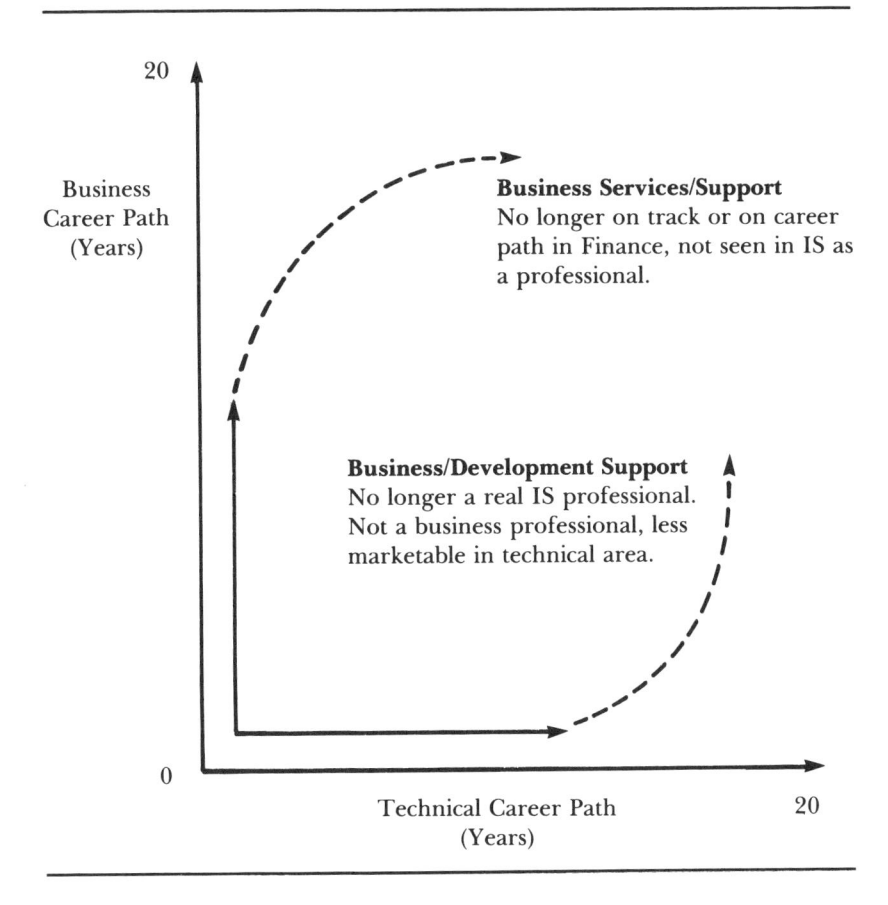

```
20 ▲
   │
Business        ┌──────────►
Career Path     │     Business Services/Support
(Years)         │     No longer on track or on career
                │     path in Finance, not seen in IS as
                │     a professional.
                │
                ▲
                │
                │   Business/Development Support    ▲
                │   No longer a real IS professional. │
                │   Not a business professional, less │
                │   marketable in technical area.     │
                │                                    │
                │                              ─────┘
                │
 0 └────────────────────────────►
              Technical Career Path          20
                   (Years)
```

hybrids. Just as Development and Business Support within IS balances technical fluency and business literacy, technically illiterate business managers are no longer effective in key positions.

It is largely too late for 40-year-olds to get lateral development. This means making a senior IS project leader a neophyte finance analyst or a senior finance executive a bungling pseudoprogrammer. The ideal time for the cross-cultural assignment is 2–3 years after the entry-level position, when the individual has learned the IS craft or functional area basics. A six-month to two-year transfer is early enough not to disturb career development and late enough to build on proven mainstream skills. When the person returns to home base, he or she is credible in both cultures and adds something special and valuable in his or her career trajectory. We need to note that unless senior management endorses or even enforces this very new philosophy of lateral development, people will have minimal incentive to make the move and maximum career ambiguity in doing so.

Education

Most IS professionals are undereducated for their roles, old or new. Perhaps they need to be treated more like machines. Firms look after computing and communications machinery very well. They generate forecasts, monitor products, and spend substantial amounts of money on maintenance. Firms need to maintain IS people, too; one form of maintenance is in education. It is essential for IS professionals to avoid depreciating their skill base. Three types of education can be related to an individual's role and career trajectory:

> Maintenance: "I need to know about this to keep up in my job."
> Development: "I must acquire this knowledge to move ahead in my career."
> Innovation: "This is not something everyone in my job needs but is important for my own personal growth."

Education programs for IS people need to be individually determined for a number of reasons: new roles; few precedents for promotion and career development; the breadth of skills, technologies, and applications they imply; and the lack of any standard career path and hence education program. What, for example, is the career path for the applications programmer who has moved into a Development Support role in an Information Center? What does he or she need to know? The job has never existed before, and will be shaped by the individual's initiative, personality, and ability.

Very roughly, maintenance education primarily relates to updates on emerging technologies; education on business basics; and design, development, and implementation methods. Development education is more concerned with advanced technical training for Technical Service roles and management education for Support roles. The education has to be provided before it is needed in the individual's work.

ROLES AND SKILL BASE FOR THE IS ORGANIZATION

Many IS project leaders acquire management skills through trial-and-error or ad hoc learning. They often recognize that they lack managerial skills and even managerial attitudes.

Exhibit 1-8 lists some examples of education topics needed to build the new IS cadre. For someone in Business Support, a program on managing change and on understanding the human side of systems (the topic on technology and people, for example), is good maintenance. For someone in Development Support, the topic is not so immediately relevant but it may be needed later as Development Education. The same topic may be irrelevant to most professionals in Technical Services but may be an innovative option for, say, a database specialist interested in trying to work with Marketing to use data modelling as a tool for product development. (This example is especially relevant to financial services and airlines where "products" are increasingly information-based).

Exhibit 1-8. Education Topics for New Roles

Suggested Topic Areas	Maintenance?	Development?	Innovation?
Technology and people			
Digital telecommunications			
Practical state of the art in network management			
Development productivity tools			
Selecting a fourth-generation language			
Business data modelling			
Systems management skills			
The effective consultant			
Architecture and integration			
Competitive uses of IT			
Financial dynamics of IT			

TRANSFORMING THE IS ORGANIZATION

Case Study: Royal Bank of Canada

The Royal Bank of Canada (RBC) is an organization that recognizes education as a critical resource for ensuring that the people side of the planning for and use of information systems is meshed with the technical. The Bank's education resources and expertise are well-established and sustained. It is currently implementing education and human resource development activities relating to information technology. The range of these specific programs fall under two main headings:

1. Career development and education for Systems staff;
2. Management technology education.

These programs support RBC's corporate strategic plan, in which "aggressive" use of technology is a stated aim. The pace of change directly or indirectly stimulated by RBC's information technology is already accelerating and it can only accelerate more.

The Bank has already shown its commitment to technology education through its Technology Management Course, attended by nearly 200 senior managers over an 18-month period. The main aim of the course is to build management awareness of the business importance of technology and to alert managers to the need to play an active role in decisions about it.

Within Operations and Systems at RBC, senior managers are strongly aware that O&S faces a period of extremely rapid changes in its mission. The O&S unit is now a business service rather than a builder of technical artifacts. Ironically, its historical excellence in technical aspects of its work is a barrier to bridging the culture gap with a business community that sees O&S as a builders of "cadillacs" and "fortress systems"!

Although the O&S unit has been isolated from the mainstream of the business, it is moving toward becoming a partner with the business units in developing products, in providing support for customer services, and in facilitating improvements in efficiency and effectiveness across all aspects of the bank's operations. The need to change is fully recognized and several initiatives are already under way to help O&S people contribute to its repositioning.

There can be no doubt whatsoever that people will be as critical—if not more so—to the successful response to business and technological changes as "strategy," investment choices, and selection of applications. It will be hard for O&S to help its systems professionals develop the new business-centered and organizational skills they need for a new era. It may be as hard for business managers at senior and middle levels to acquire computer fluency: comfort with their understanding, not so much of technology, but of the decision-making process concerning it, and with their own role in the deployment and use of technology.

To help solve the problems within O&S at RBC, senior managers have put substantial effort into defining a vision of O&S and identifying how to move towards a very new style of operating while retaining the value of the old skills and experience. They have also made progress in analyzing career development needs using the roles analysis framework described earlier in this chapter, and have initiated important organizational changes—such as creating a new account management position—aimed at building a strong partnership with business units.

If RBC is to continue to adapt successfully to a changing market it will need to make fairly substantial additional investments in education and career development. The economic rationale is a simple one: the skills, attitudes, and mutual understanding of people in O&S and their business partners will be the determining factor in getting business value from the growing systems investment.

The shift in RBC has not in any way been a routine task; tensions remain strong. The challenge is to support existing strengths, break open old mind sets, encourage shifts in attitude and behavior, and provide fast, comprehensive maintenance. Anything less is to fall behind.

Virtually every respected commentator on the past, present, and coming experience with IT in large firms highlights the management of organizational change as the critical success factor. Many firms will spend the same amount of money on technology but only a few may get the same value.

This is apparent from the past few years' explosive growth in expenditures on office automation—where some firms have seen real economic gains and others very little benefit—and from studies of the difference in cost and quality of computer systems. The variation between the firms that have positioned their professionals for new roles in a new technical environment versus the laggards is 3 to 1 or more. This variation translates to a cost difference of $20 million versus $60 million and a time difference of 40 months versus 120 months for a large system to meet competitive needs. A lack of support from middle management is increasingly seen as the reason many aggressive business and technical strategies for using IT have had far less success than expected.

Career development planning and education are not panaceas, but properly designed and delivered they can provide direct economic benefit if they resolve any of these now-standard problems intrinsic to IT. The RBC recognizes this and is adding extra momentum to its use of education to support its business strategy for technology and to create the management processes, partnerships, and actions to turn strategy into business benefit. The RBC's actions are only the first exemplars of what will be the trend in the late 1980s.

Barriers to Education

IS professionals need to spend 10 percent of their time, half a day a week, on education. They rarely do so, because of many barriers:

- Logistics: They are too busy to take three days to two weeks off from work to attend a course.
- Quality: The vast range of available external courses vary widely in quality and it is hard to assess them from the brochures.
- Topics: Courses are rarely well-tailored to the individual's needs.
- Management: Access to education for junior people in IS often depends on the importance their supervisors place on education and on monitoring their own staff's development. Also, proper performance appraisal is a neglected and even unrespected supervisory responsibility in many IS units.
- Cost: Quality education is expensive in terms of direct costs and the indirect ones of travel and time away.

These barriers can be removed by:

- An explicit policy requiring all IS professionals to spend 10 percent of their time on education.
- A formal plan for education based on individuals' stated needs in terms of maintenance, development and innovation, their supervisors' assessments, their role definitions (as in Exhibit 2–3), and a survey of the best education programs being provided by universities, vendors, and consulting firms.
- Over the long term, the use of information technology to improve the logistics and cost of education through video-conferencing, which is underexploited as a vehicle for accelerated education. Video-con-

ROLES AND SKILL BASE FOR THE IS ORGANIZATION

ferencing reduces travel and scheduling demands, allows the cost of education to be shared by a number of units (or firms) through point-to-multipoint communications, and allows the far-too-small supply of top rate educators to reach a wider audience.

Summary: Recommendations for Action

Repositioning the IS organization now for its new, broad, business-focused mission is essential. The ability of firms to exploit IT depends increasingly on people—not money, hardware, software, or tools. The key steps to take are these:

1. Bring telecommunications and information systems together into an overall information services organization if that has not already been done.
2. Perform a baseline analysis of the roles implicit in the firm's business plan and explicit in the IS mission and its capital project portfolio.
3. Use the role definitions to (a) establish the equal importance and prestige of maintenance and operations; (b) to give clear signals to IS staff about the new skills they must build with support from management through lateral development and education and (c) to give clear signals about the new expectations for service, performance, and career development that the roles imply.
4. Encourage IS professionals to think about their own skill base, education needs, and career trajectory.
5. Set up a process for lateral development and movement into and out of IS.
6. Set up a process for internal recruitment.
7. Reevaluate entry-level recruiting (and recruiters) in relation to role needs.
8. Establish an ongoing education plan with the responsibility for it clearly defined; this is not a part-time or ad hoc assignment.
9. Recognize that the middle-level IS managers and project leaders are likely to be a major roadblock to change. They have moved through an obsolescent technocentric career path, lack management education, are often unconvinced or even ignorant of the need to shift from a focus on traditional systems development to service and partnership with users, and lack knowledge about

TRANSFORMING THE IS ORGANIZATION

emerging technologies, end user tools, and user-centered or user-managed project development methods. Getting these people to agree with the principles and recommendations made here is a priority; it may not be easy. A prerequisite is to make sure they get education in the basics of management and of business.

CHAPTER TWO

RELATIONSHIP OF SENIOR MANAGEMENT AND THE IS ORGANIZATION

PETER G.W. KEEN

The goal of any information services organization must be to create a management process for using information technologies—telecommunications, computers, workstations, and multimedia data—as a co-ordinated business resource. The barriers to achieving this are generally not knowledge or budgets or technology but the politics of ambiguity.

- The gap between authority and responsibility that creates ambiguity around who decides rather than what is to be decided;
- The lack of clarity about the new role of IS given its historical role and its distance from centrality in the organization;
- The historical emphasis on managing IS by delegation rather than by senior management's direct and overt oversight;
- The insularity of IS in its relationships and contacts across the organization, and the insularity of management in its handling of the business implications of IT and IT management.

These are the agenda items for the IS manager in his or her relationships with peers and seniors in line and corporate functions.

Managing IS as a business service function has no precedents. Historically IS has been treated differently from other areas of business and in many ways IS reinforces its difference by emphasizing itself as a major competitive force in business. As "data processing" IS was different and unimportant, part of corporate overhead. As MIS it became more important but was still different; management looked for MIS professionals who could outline strategic plans that went beyond automating back office functions. Management supported its MIS people but failed to provide any new authority; an MIS manager had to make a case for increased budgets, and had to recapture funding through cost allocations. The MIS manager's political currency was influence, not authority.

Now IS is clearly seen as important; a new term, *Chief Information Officer* (CIO), reflects the new importance, even though it may only be a fashion whose vogue will generate a backlash. In any case, the CIO is vaguely defined; there is after all no Chief Marketing Officer title though there is a Chief Financial Officer and a Chief Operating Officer. The title suggests that IS is still different. It is not embedded in the firm's management process and management tradition.

Integrating IS and the business management process is much more difficult than technically integrating telecommunications and computing; without established precedents the problems of ambiguity and insularity make IS intensely political.

The problem has to be faced head on; there is no quick fix. Without senior management's recognition of the issues, an IS manager can make only incremental moves. That is acceptable only if the IS manager is not trying to use IT to create or support radical business and organizational change.

Authority Versus Responsibility

Exhibit 2-1 summarizes the IS manager's main political dilemma. Each quadrant identifies a stereotypical IS role.

Exhibit 2-1. Stereotypical Management Roles

	Authority Low	Authority High
Responsibility High	Whipping Post	Information Executive
Responsibility Low	Information Janitor	Monopolist

RELATIONSHIP OF SENIOR MANAGEMENT

The *Whipping Post* is the IS manager who recognizes the need to define an organization-wide plan for deploying IT and seeks to take on the following new level of responsibility.

- To be an advocate for meshing IT with the firm's strategic business plans;
- To define the standards and policies that move IS away from fragmented systems and towards an integrated information utility.

The Whipping Post's responsibility is not backed by authority. Standards and policies lack teeth. Real authority lies with the business unit manager who has the lowest level of responsibility for profit and loss. The IS manager's strategy is aggressive and proactive but the dialogue with the business managers is reactive and easily becomes defensive.

The *Monopolist*, by contrast, has the authority but does not make any effort to play a coordinating role or to add a technician's view into the business. This is the old line data processing manager who for decades controlled all aspects of computing resources, including an effective veto over the use of outside services. The Monopolist fought personal computers and lived by control and allocations.

The *Information Janitors* have neither authority nor responsibility. They run a tight shop and focus on quality of operations. Any use of IT for business innovation is irrelevant and they do not intrude on anyone else's political turf.

The *Information Executive*, whether grandiloquently entitled CIO or simply Vice President of Information Systems, has the necessary political clout and the business and organizational responsibility to balance the joint trend towards

1. Central direction of the main infrastructures and enabling systems (particularly the backbone communications network), the priority data resources, and the key standards for phasing the move towards technical integration;
2. Decentralized development and use of IT, especially in the areas of personal computing, end user computing, and office technology and customer service applications.

The Whipping Post's position is very difficult. He or she is creating plans that require these two trends to move together, but unless senior management clarifies the question of "who decides?" rather than "what do we decide?" political tension is guaranteed. Also guaranteed are IS's frustration, and users' rejection of IS's right to make initiatives for corporate purposes that intrude on their territory or affect their autonomy.

Obviously, the Whipping Post cannot simply reinstate the old monopoly in a new context with an even bigger budget. If line managers are unresponsive to the Whipping Post, they will hardly welcome an information czar. That in itself may be a strong reason for any IS manager to avoid being crippled politically by a CIO position title.

Clarifying the importance of meshing authority with responsibility is essential, but the case can be made effectively by tackling another area of ambiguity: the mission of IS. Quite simply, IS has no inherent right to a powerful new mandate and corporate oversight; these need to be justified in business terms.

Clarifying the IS Mission

It has become increasingly clear that IT can be used strategically in a firm only where senior management's statement of vision provides a context for planning. The statement underlies deploying scarce capital for IT investments rather than for some other priority and gives a reason for taking a global view of IS versus the more normal department-by-department and project-by-project perspective.

When General Electric Chairman of the Board Jack Welch stated "We're out to make sure that GE uses computer technology more effectively than anybody else in the world," he was providing his Manager of Corporate Information Systems, John Cunningham, the corporate vision around which to build his IS mission. In 1985 that mission involved close to a billion-dollar investment by GE on computing and telecommunications and a projected 1990 IS budget of two billion dollars. (*Infosystems,* December 1985, pp. 32–37.)

This kind of vision is a direction for business rather than a plan. It is needed because of the long lead times for IT innovation, and because product and market initiatives based on IT create radical changes in work, the selling process, relationships, and even organizational structures. Such initiatives disturb the status quo and intrude on stable practices, assumptions, and territories.

Senior management needs to focus on its business vision in order for IT to be managed as a strategic, business entity and a priority contender for capital, instead of being treated as a tactical, technical expense. The IS management can then define the mission that corresponds to the vision, thus clarifying the issue of authority.

Historically, IS has not had a mission embedded in the wider management process of the firm. It has been a builder of systems and operator of facilities. Its relationships with its users have been more like master/servant or priesthood/laity rather than like a partnership between equals. Defined as an expense item, IS has been part of the organizational overhead; it has a function, not a mission.

A mission requires a fundamental shift in mind set within IS. Technology and the ability to make technology work are the means, not the ends. The end is a business accomplishment that would not occur without a mission. The mission statement has to define that end in those terms and align management support, not just at the top but among the line executives who are the main users of IS's services. The components of a mission are

- A consensually meaningful and organizationally credible statement of the business drivers for IS;
- An identification of the "news";
- A practical philosophy for creating a partnership and managing a dialogue with the user community.

The natural starting point for the statement of business drivers is one to avoid: a collection of cliches about using IT for competitive advantage. The stories on which those cliches were built were part of a process of awareness building and propaganda to get business managers to think about IT in new terms. The many case studies of success—American Airlines, American Hospital Supply, and more recently, Federal Express—were striking claims for managerial attention.

They still remain so, but skeptics can argue that those are special instances—that while IT is certainly relevant to competitive plans and options, it has been oversold. The best counter to this criticism may simply be to focus on IT and competitive disadvantage: to look at the ways some industries have redefined their base level of service with electronic delivery and coordination and to conclude that no firm can afford to fall behind such pacesetters. This approach defines the IT mission in terms of supporting the firm's business thrust, especially on the vital priority of focusing on technology to build and keep customer loyalty. The result is IS's relation to the business less in terms of strategic innovation and more in terms of participating in areas of the business that are critical survival factors in a volatile marketplace.

Reviewing the history of using IT for competitive advantage shows that the noted exemplar firms benefited most in the area of capturing

TRANSFORMING THE IS ORGANIZATION

the customer in basic transactions. For example, American Airlines' Sabre program, the first of the now ubiquitous computer reservation systems, involved very little that was new. The airline didn't change service, alter routes, or attempt to squeeze in additional seats. It merely developed the most efficient way of handling its core transactions: an order entry system for travel agents. Similarly, American Hospital Supply's legendary system was a new way of handling the company's most basic transactions: sales calls to hospitals and placing orders.

To clarify the legitimacy of IS authority and the basis for partnership, a mission has to relate to the core business drivers and must be recognizable to anyone in the firm as justifying new rules of management for and with IS. Both the Royal Bank of Canada and Citibank Latino have demonstrated this ability to create an IS mission built around the core business. In order for IS to effect and accelerate the core business drivers, IS must be able to discern the "news," differentiating acceptable IT applications from "gee whiz" prototypes.

We are in an era of overblown promises about information; too many statements about IT in the business and computer press ignore the tough details of implementation and long lead times IS intrinsically involves, and "technobabble" substitutes for concreteness and practicality. For IS to talk about its mission in terms of productivity, offices of the future, competitive advantage, etc., now gets at best a ho-hum response and at worst an "oh yeah?". At the same time, beneath the noise is a business message that matters to everyone in the firm, a message that must be there if IS is to claim special attention from management. There has to be some "news." This point is illustrated by John Watson, head of Information Management for British Airlines, who pioneered automated reservations systems—BOADICEA predates any U.S. system and its successor BABS (British Airways Booking System) has been a 20-year evolution from it. Watson points out that in the late 1960s it was news to talk about using computer terminals to confirm airline bookings instantly. Later on it was news to suggest that a travel agent could make reservations directly.

What is the news now? Not expert systems, telecommunications, the power of personal computers, or the promise of office technology, but a concrete statement of the special contribution IS offers. The news is not a plan. Many IS organizations are good at planning. They can provide managers with lengthy and well-written summaries of application plans, major projects, technology trends, capital expenditures, and budgets, but planning can cloud rather than clarify the mission and obscure the news.

This takes us to the most important element of the IS mission: the philosophy of partnership. The philosophy is expressed in decisions about formal structure, but the decisions are effect not cause. How will IS relate to its clients, colleagues, and users? In large firms who are leaders in business, technical, and organizational aspects of IS the trend is towards

- Adopting a philosophy based on account management and marketing, with service and support the new ethic rather than the building and running of systems and facilities.
- Distributing development to business units, often with a form of matrix management where divisional IS units report to corporate IS and to the business unit manager. The divisional unit may be either physically located with its users or—a more cautious choice—still remain with the main IS unit but with a clearly defined support and service role.
- Moving away from basing the relationship on budgets and cost-based allocations towards some form of quasi-profit center, where prices replace costs and user managers have options about sources and levels of service. The old monopoly becomes a regulated free market.

Whatever the choices about structure and accounting, IS has to send a strong signal about how it intends to behave—will it be a real vendor, a corporate support unit, or a consultant? Will the master/serf relationship—where what IS does is set by agreed-on budgets and deliverables—disappear, along with the priest/laity one—where IS controls the trade-offs between cost, time, and technology? This latter relationship with users is often criticized as the "Cadillac syndrome," where "the trouble with systems is they give us Cadillacs that take years to build when we just want a Chevy, now."

The IS leadership has to view the mission as a priority. Changes in organization are an outcome of the mission, not the reverse. The process of clarifying the mission has two audiences:

- The external world of business units and clients for whom the outputs of the process establish unambiguously the basis for partnership and the value of the IS services and strategy;
- The internal IS unit itself in which many, often most, of the experienced professionals may be the main obstacle to change. Their career path and background have emphasized technical skills, systems development, control, and traditional project management

methodologies that focus on technical work rather than business orientation.

Ending the Tradition of Senior Management Delegation

Delegation is not a strategy. More and more firms are heeding that message. Whether or not IT is a force for competitive advantage or the new base for efficiency of operations and effectiveness of service, it is a growing component of the company's capital commitments. It involves frequent business risk, frequent technical risk, organizational stress, long lead times, complex project management, and difficult details of implementation. It has to be directed from the top.

Although the need for direction from the top ought to be obvious, the history of IS encourages delegation because of a notion that it is so different from any other organizational function that no precedents are available to guide senior management. It is fair to say that senior executives simply do not feel that they have valid intuitions about IS. Too often they rely on written, formal plans and fall back on established cost-based justifications, thus creating a barrier to management action.

Three factors can end delegation and create a new management partnership in which IS managers and line executives together are responsible for a business deliverable. These are:

- An industry context of opportunity, threat, volatility or vacuum that opens a new business-oriented perspective on IT;
- A top management team that provides a focused statement of vision;
- A management forum where the business and IS leadership can create momentum for shared action.

Although IS managers cannot greatly influence the first two of these factors (except through informal mechanisms for dialogue with senior business executives), the third area is one of strong potential leverage.

One fairly fashionable approach is to set up IS "steering committees." These can be effective if they focus on building awareness and briefing business leaders on critical issues rather than on detailed IS plans. Sears' rules for the Advisory Board to its telecommunications organization (a separate service company) provide a useful summary of the principles for such committees.

- The purpose of the meetings is mainly to build a shared understanding. (Many steering committees begin their existence with reviews of IS plans and then quickly recognize they need to shift to briefings that help de-obfuscate the plans and that raise the level of attention from projects and budgets to business criteria and trade-offs, especially those involving priorities, lead time and people resources.)
- There are no formal votes and one goal is to avoid getting into situations where there has to be an appeal to a referee.
- The Board includes officers of the individual business groups who have the seniority and influence to represent their business unit's views and to be listened to when they return to the unit.
- The Board handles the negotiations that are a natural aspect of joint planning as an integral part of working together, so that "political" work is carried out in a cooperative way, directly and to open resolution, impasse, compromise, or consensus.
- The Advisory Board members are the ambassadors to their own business unit committees and management planning and decision-making fora. This is how IS gets away from the old political arguments where it lacks authority. The Advisory Board provides clout and credibility.

With the right level of membership and appropriate briefings and rules of behavior, such committees are an essential step in getting rid of political ambiguity.

Obviously, the nature of the membership in such a group is critical. Citibank coined the term "the Gang of Seven" to describe the group that gave clout and impetus to its international telecommunications plans. That group also later generated some disastrous decisions when it overlooked the importance of being well-briefed before making major decisions involving unproven technology, but in its early years it created immense energy and credibility for the technical staff's plans and implementation.

The individuals named to the Gang of Seven were the signal to the organization that this was not going to be yet another committee. The members were recognized as movers and leaders, expected to provide the bank with aggressive new products and market strategies. No one in the organization needed to be told that senior management now viewed telecommunications as a central part of the firm's business strategy. No management memos or high level mandates would have had the same impact if the committee membership had included people who lacked influence and centrality in the business.

The problem of political clout is a central one for IS. The following available options do not resolve the issue of clarifying ambiguity and legitimizing authority.

1. Recreate the monopoly and get a mandate. If anything, this compounds the problem of delegation. Without the type and level of ambassador the Sears Advisory Board and Citibank Gang employ, IS has to fight its own political battles dealing with unbriefed managers instead of ones who have been part of the thinking process.
2. Avoid the problem and stay with the Whipping Post role. The problem remains the same.
3. Push the problem on to the user managers. That abandons any effort to mesh authority with responsibility or, worse, abdicates responsibility. Senior management delegation ends with getting a statement of vision and creating a suitable management forum.

Ending Organizational Insularity

All the actions and mechanisms described above play a part in helping to end insularity, not just inside IS or between IS and users, but across every area relevant to using IT, whether for innovation in customer service, improved organizational efficiency, or meeting competitors' moves.

Insularity is often a result of several sets of circumstances:

- Senior business managers are often too far away from the firm's customers and take too narrow a view of "competition." Many banks have been preempted in the use of IT in ways that have created substantial competitive disadvantage for them. They were unfamiliar with the ways third-party competitors were using IT to intrude on their traditional territory.

  These predictable, but too often overlooked, competitors have included companies like American Express, Sears, Merrill Lynch, and Geisco; multinationals such as Volvo, British Petroleum, and Mobil, who used the banks' technology to help them set up their own in-house banks; and Florida supermarkets who have taken over point of sale from the state banks who thought they would control it.

The same has been true in the airline business, where the traditional players now find that Dun and Bradstreet in the United States and ABC internationally are taking control of their distribution networks even while the airlines pay them to display the schedule data that is the base for D&B's and ABC's independent home travel reservation systems.

A company's management insularity is often the main reason other firms have surpassed them. The people at the top here do not recognize how quickly the rules of business can be changed by (a) a combination of deregulation or the expectation of deregulation; (b) sophisticated consumers responsive to convenience of service and ease of access to the firm; (c) telecommunications as the vehicle for adding new services; and (d) customer data as the base for cross-selling products and capturing the customer relationship.

- IS leaders manage in terms of a technocentric mind set and isolation from the organization's needs, processes, and priorities. This type of insularity, reflected in today's IS organization, is the reason we have to think through how to move quickly and firmly to build from first principles for tomorrow's organization.
- Business units now have more personal computers than filing cabinets but they are still unlikely to have formal business plans for IT or realize that they need to take an active management role.
- IS and business units each operate in separate worlds, with different vocabularies and blurred understandings of each other.

One of the IS manager's primary objectives has to be to end insularity. A major vehicle for doing so is education, targeted not to train people about technology but to increase awareness and then to turn awareness into action. Senior management education is the fastest growing part of the IS budget in many leading firms. The aim is to alert managers to what IT is doing to the competitive dynamics of their industry and to help them identify opportunities. A more recent trend is to help IS professionals broaden their perspective and extend their skills to add functional/business and organizational/personal abilities to their technical ones. Business units also need briefings both on what IS means to their management process and on what they should do to get business benefit from the technology they have.

No IS manager can afford to be without an education plan, which is the human resource R&D. Just as computer vendors who cut back on R&D can boost profits in the short term, IS organizations that neglect education sacrifice a quiet life today for tomorrow's energy, innovation, and knowledge base.

Education is of course not the only way to end insularity. Enterprising IS managers can help break it down through almost every organizational mechanism discussed in this chapter:

- Education;
- Distributing development;
- Building end user support teams and other bridgeheads such as information centers;
- Steering committees;
- An account management or marketing-based organizational structure;
- Informal relationships;
- Project management and development methods that focus on the user's perspective rather than on structuring the technical work. Prototypes and such user-led project techniques as IBM Canada's JAD (Joint Application Development) are examples.

Whatever the mechanism, insularity is the barrier to building the IS organization of tomorrow and IS managers must take every opportunity to end it.

Conclusion: Mutuality

The relationship between IS and business managers has to be one of mutual understanding—not of the details of each other's activities, knowledge, and skill base, but of the other's needs, constraints, and contributions to an organizational venture partnership. This coresponsiveness of equals, where negotiation, facilitation and IS service, plus business unit targeting of opportunity and priority, takes the place of separation of functions and imbalance of responsibility and authority.

This last point is illustrated in Exhibit 2-2, which can be overlaid on Exhibit 2-1 to summarize what has to be created to ensure that IS resolves ambiguity and organizational instability. Exhibit 2-3 combines the two preceding exhibits.

The Missionary and Whipping Post are often the same. The Missionary is ahead of the business leadership and hence is unlikely to have been able to get authority but takes on responsibility. The Foot-

Exhibit 2-2. Roles in the IS Organization

	Business Leadership	
	Passive, Reactive	Active, Innovative
IS Leadership Active, Innovative	Missionary	Information Executive
Passive, Reactive	Loser	Footdragger

Exhibit 2-3. Relationship Between IS and Business Managers

	IS has Low Authority, Business Leadership is Passive	High Authority, Business Leadership is Active
IS has High Responsibility, Leads Actively	Whipping Post Missionary	Information Executive
IS has Low Responsibility, is Passive	Information Janitor Loser	Monopolist Footdragger

dragger and Monopolist are also often equivalent, with both of them not recognizing the new business responsibility of IT in supporting line units. The Loser and Information Janitor are amiably content with well-run data centers and no backlogs (which means no customers looking for service) and no projects in trouble (i.e., no risks taken and no innovation created).

The Information Executive has balanced authority and responsibility, and has the business leadership setting a pace and challenge to which he or she responds.

To succeed in overcoming the politics of ambiguity and insularity, IS and the rest of the organization must evolve a synergistic relationship that focuses equally on the overall corporate strategy and recognizes information as a resource to be exploited in ways very different from the past.

CHAPTER THREE

BUILDING RELATIONSHIPS THROUGHOUT THE CORPORATE ENTITY

ROBERT W. ZMUD

We are moving into an era in which most of an organization's work groups have both the capability and the motivation to plan for, acquire, and implement their own information systems.[1] Unfortunately, the relationships between and among these work groups and the IS organization tend to become murky at best and hostile at worst. What should be the nature of the relationships between the IS unit and these other organizational units? Once defined, how can the relationships be built and sustained? It is likely that most IS organizations will commit, or already have committed, considerable energy to examining these two questions.

A useful way of framing this problem is to view the introduction of information technology into an organization as a technology transfer process. Here, the IS organization is seen to serve a research and development role: it maintains an awareness of new information technologies and of where competitors stand regarding these technologies and it develops prototypes of new information products and services. It also works with other units in applying these information products and services to improve or expand the organization's product and services as well as its operational and managerial work systems.

The advantage of framing the issue of relationships with this view is that we already have considerable knowledge on how to successfully manage R&D activities. For example, successful R&D projects are invariably managed as follows:

1. A problem or opportunity is recognized.
2. A possible resolution of the problem, or exploitation of the opportunity, is recognized through a new technology.

TRANSFORMING THE IS ORGANIZATION

3. A champion for this new technology emerges and begins to "sell" others on its merits.
4. This champion locates a sponsor, who provides necessary resources and political support.
5. The decision to "adopt" this technical solution is based on a careful, *risk/return* analysis. In other words, two basic ideas are recognized.
    - New technologies cannot be treated generically; high-risk investments are fine as long as they have the potential to produce high returns.
    - The investment decisions for new technologies should not be treated as isolated events, but rather as elements comprising an investment portfolio.
6. Full-scale implementation of an adopted technology is preceded by pilot studies, in which benefits and costs are experienced in a low-risk environment.
7. Adaptation of both the technology and adopting work units is both expected and managed.
8. Considerable training and support both precedes and accompanies the introduction of the technology.

It is useful to compare this process with the one used to implement a successful information system. On close examination, it is clear that the two processes have much in common.

Each of the events in the above list involves considerable uncertainty: Is the problem or opportunity important and well-defined? Who considers it important, and who really understands it? Is this a proven technology? Is this technology the best way to resolve the problem or exploit the opportunity? What exactly is the nature and size of the required investment? What are the political stakes for the champion? the sponsor? adopting work units? What are the business stakes for the adopting work units? How might the technology affect the organization, and what type of preparation is required to deal with these results? What are the direct and indirect benefits and costs to the organization if the project succeeds? if the project fails? How large a financial return is required to balance the risk inherent in the project? Is the pilot study a realistic trial? How much adaptation will be required with the technology in adopting work units?

With successful R&D projects, the individuals responsible for managing a project anticipate and reduce uncertainties such as these as project activities unfold (a number of project management and de-

BUILDING RELATIONSHIPS

cision aids have been developed to facilitate such management actions).[2]

Aside from project management tools and techniques, how are these uncertainties reduced? Usually, a project team is formed whose members either already have or can acquire the necessary information to manage the uncertainties. Two resources are equally critical: technology users (line managers confronted with a problem or opportunity) and technology providers (R&D managers). Line managers understand the business needs that *pull* a technology into a work unit and technology managers understand the technology they are *pushing* into the organization. The R&D efforts prove most successful when line managers and R&D managers work together in examining the appropriateness of a technology, in gathering support for the technology, and in applying it.

Based on experiences from R&D projects, the successful introduction of any new technology largely depends on the ability of mid-level line and technology managers to forge effective working relationships. Not only do these middle managers have the knowledge and experience to cope with the high levels of uncertainty associated with new technologies, but they also bring the authority and access to funds which are necessary for managing a technical change effort. Because they can marshal resources, commit the resources to innovation efforts, and gain the commitment of others, mid-level line and technology managers are the culture of the innovating organization.

Today's Information Services Context

One aspect of today's IS context makes the teamwork among line and technology managers particularly important, if not more difficult.[3] Most information products and services are targeted toward an organization's *business platform*, which is its customers, its front- and back office procedures, and its staff, managers, professionals, and management systems. The nature of this platform creates significant pressure for line managers to disperse IT resources and the decision-making responsibilities regarding these resources. However, in order for customers, managers, professionals, etc., to use information products and services, a robust *technology platform* must exist. This platform—consisting of appropriate data, processing, and communications

TRANSFORMING THE IS ORGANIZATION

capacities and architectures—builds significant pressure for IS managers to prescribe IT policies, plans, standards, and guidelines.

Technological innovation in today's IS context must be driven simultaneously within two distinct but interrelated work domains: a firm's business platform—a line management responsibility—and the firm's technology platform—an IS management responsibility. "Push" and "pull" forces operate within both of these work domains. The direction of the push-pull effort may change but it is always based on business needs. To facilitate technological innovation in the business platform, "need pull" and "technology push" are desired; to facilitate technological innovation in the technology platform, "technology pull" and "need push" are desired (see Exhibit 3-1).

Competing pressures for local autonomy and global coordination, however, often bring these two spheres of technological innovation into conflict. Line managers often feel pressed to apply nonstandard technology quickly in order to achieve or maintain a competitive position. If this technology does not fit within the current architecture, providing adequate technical support can prove difficult if not impossible.

IS managers often feel pressed to use current resources to make investments in a future technical platform. Such projects often delay or postpone requests by line managers to enhance a current business platform. Unless line and IS managers work together in facilitating innovation within both work domains, it is unlikely that the long-term intentions of either will be achieved.

The challenge of promoting technological innovation within today's IS context increases when the introduction of information products and services results in both winners and losers among an organization's managers. Line managers can gain or lose resources, responsibilities, and power depending on how organizational activities are collapsed, expanded, or shifted across departmental and organizational boundaries. IS managers can gain or lose resources, responsibilities, and power depending on how information processing activities are collapsed, expanded, or shifted.

It is hard to change people's work habits, and it is harder to get them to participate in a change effort. Harder yet is gaining any participation when someone stands to lose something in the process. The critical problem in today's IS services context thus becomes this: How can innovation be promoted in each of the two work spheres when successful innovation requires the joint efforts of both line and IS managers, but often brings the interests of each into conflict?

Exhibit 3-1. "Push-Pull" Dynamics

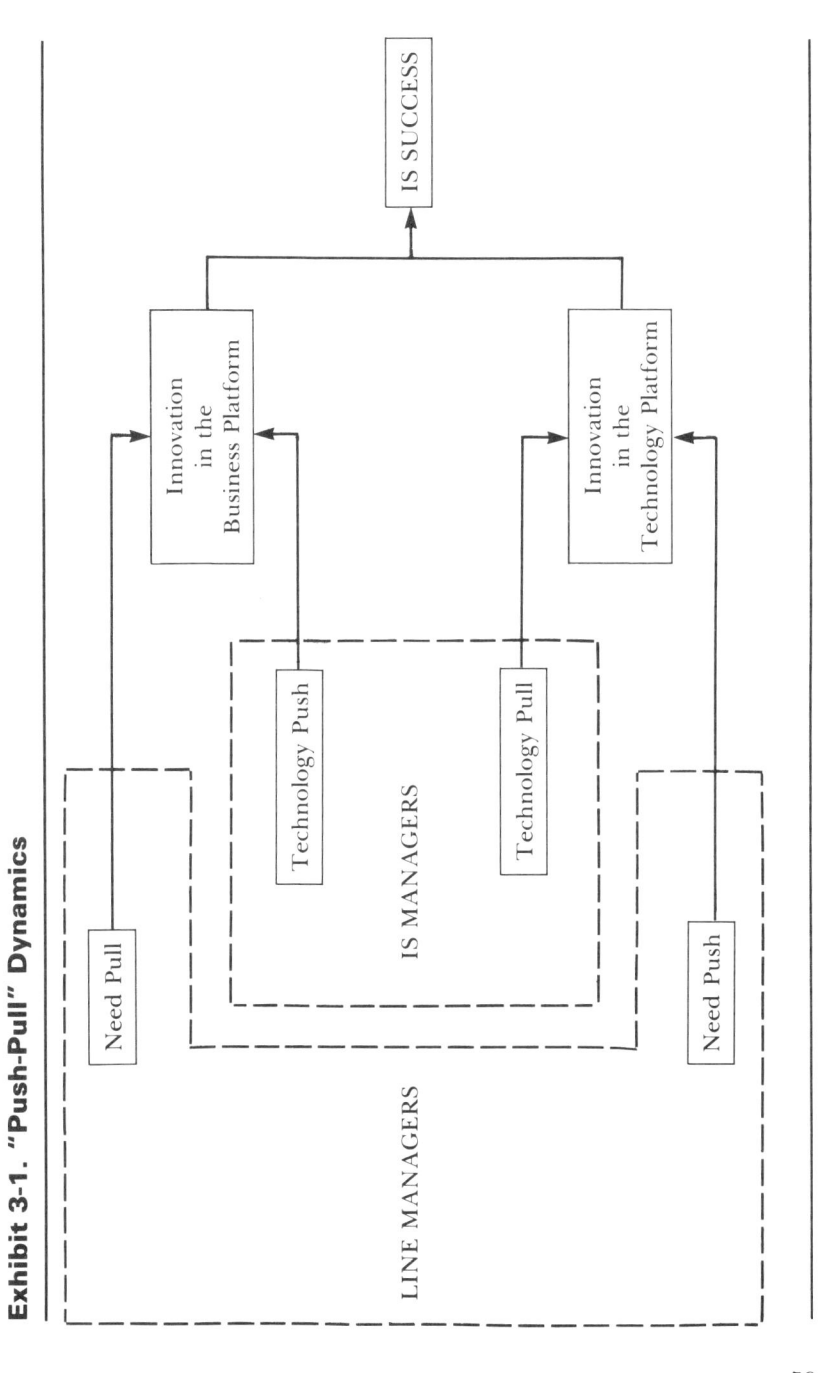

TRANSFORMING THE IS ORGANIZATION

The Freedom To Fail and To Succeed

One approach to this potentially difficult situation is to create a *freedom-to-fail* climate within the organization. In this approach an organization's members are rewarded for innovating successfully but not punished for failure as long as their innovative efforts were based on informed risks. The view espoused by Citicorp is worth remembering: "Failures are part of the landscape if you're trying to change things and grow."[4] Without the freedom to fail, even an informed risk becomes too great.

This freedom-to-fail climate alone, however, is insufficient. It is unreasonable to expect managers to commit themselves to efforts that introduce new information products or services if they anticipate a personal loss. Consider the following example: Substantial personnel costs, with reductions in both managerial and clerical staff as well as the operating budget, might be anticipated in a Customer Services department upon the introduction of a software product that enables customers to obtain answers to shipping and warranty questions by directly tying into the firm's computer. Any effort to develop this software product must involve Customer Services staff as well as IS personnel knowledgeable of current Customer Service applications. For such individuals to commit themselves to this development effort, they must have the *freedom-to-succeed*. That is, they must believe that their organizational situations, e.g., compensation, advancement potential, and status, will be enhanced, not lessened, through the product's success.

How does one establish an organization characterized by the freedom to fail and the freedom to succeed? Experts suggest a number of strategies:

1. Managers must be given the responsibility to innovate. The need to pursue innovative ideas must be built into job descriptions and structures.
2. Managers must be given the permission to pursue innovative ideas. Scanning the environment, developing ideas, and talking with others about these ideas takes both time and effort.
3. Managers should have available sites for experimentation. Innovation can disrupt normal organizational activities, and managers may be unwilling to risk ongoing vendor, customer, or interdepartmental relationships. This roadblock to innovation can be avoided by providing cooperative or low-risk sites for experimentation.

4. Managers should have access to multiple funding sources. Given the uncertainties involved with technological innovation, it is difficult to predict both the outcome of a project and others' reactions to a project proposal. Having access to multiple funding sources thus creates alternatives.
5. Managers must be recognized for their efforts to innovate. Engaging in innovative behaviors risks reputations. If a manager cannot obtain positive feedback for innovative behavior, it is unlikely that it will continue.
6. Managers should be compensated for their successes as innovators and as sponsors of innovative activities. Placing one's reputation on the line, where failure is more likely than success, has to be strongly motivated. Cash awards or royalties, even if they are nominal, are effective motivators.
7. Managers must be provided with opportunities for career advancement. By its nature, innovation disrupts organizational activities and redefines organizational roles. If individuals are unable to envision themselves beyond their current roles, it is unlikely that they will initiate a sequence of events that might diminish or eliminate these roles.

Establishing Partnership Relations Between Line and Information Services Managers

The difficulties inherent in efforts to promote technological innovation within the two work domains of today's IS context suggest that successful innovation is most likely to occur when it is planned, used, and cooperative. New information products and services must fit within the existing and future technology platform, and innovations for the technology platform should neither constrain existing products and services nor deter future ones. For that reason, innovation must be planned. Innovations must also be used, because it is only after experimenting with one information product or service within a specific business situation that truly significant information products or services can be envisioned. Finally, what is required is not innovation per se, but "cooperative" innovation between line and IS managers.

Such cooperation is engendered when line and IS managers establish *partnership relations*. These relationships exist when line and IS managers become equal partners in the business of the organization, jointly concerned with the organization's products and services, and both responsible for business success.

What exactly is the nature of the business climate created by establishing partnership relations? Travelers Corporation provides a good example:[5] Every morning, key IS managers, users, customers, and vendors get together via teleconferencing to review the previous day's performance. Because everyone is instantly accountable for what happened the previous day, the sessions enable each member of Travelers' IS management team to identify problems and opportunities, and to recognize exactly who in their total business environment has the capability and authority to help them resolve a problem or exploit an opportunity.

Two aspects of partnership relations cannot be overemphasized: their personal and intertwining natures. Partnership relations do not emerge overnight. Rather, they develop over time through the frequent interactions, both work-related and social, of organizational equals who respect and trust one another. For example, IS management cannot ask business units to address IT issues in their business planning and then become upset when a business unit hires an IS planner. Likewise, line management cannot expect IS management to adopt a more business-oriented posture and then become upset when IS personnel begin developing working relationships with customers.

Making Partnership Relations Work

Three factors are essential in building successful partnership relations among an organization's line and IS managers. First, senior management must encourage, nurture, and support the development of these relationships. Second, line and IS managers must individually engage in a variety of actions across both work domains. Third, managerial mechanisms must be implemented that both promote and sustain these relationships.

Senior Management Roles

The previous chapter focused on the nature of the relationships between an organization's IS executives and other members of the senior management team. Here, the concern is with the actions taken by senior managers to induce their subordinates to engage in innovative behaviors. Specifically, senior managers need to:

1. Provide a vision that directs innovative efforts;
2. Actively promote these efforts;
3. Fiscally and politically sponsor promising projects.

A senior management vision of an organization's future strategies and of the role that IT will play in these strategies identifies for subordinates those business activities likely to benefit from information products and services, as well as the information technologies required to implement the products and services. Two aspects of such a vision are particularly important:

1. The vision must be communicated to all of an organization's managers.
2. The vision should clarify the desired organizational posture within each of the marketplaces in which the organization currently competes or anticipates competing in the future.

Because of its direct and indirect costs, innovation must be targeted. Senior management vision is an extremely effective means of directing middle managers' attention to key business concerns.

In addition to articulating the vision, senior managers must actively promote—through their influence in establishing an organization's climate—innovation by middle managers. The seven strategies listed earlier provide a good checklist for assessing the extent to which an organization's climate is conducive to managerial innovation. A good illustration of what can be done to promote innovation is the 3M policy whereby division managers are given an end-of-the-year bonus if 25 percent of their division's revenue comes from products introduced within the previous five years.[6] Only senior managers have both the authority and the influence to fabricate work environments characterized by these seven strategies.

Finally, senior managers must be willing to personally sponsor well-conceived, innovative projects regardless of the organizational source of a project. Here, sponsorship refers to political actions that build support or overcome resistance, venture capital activities, and the willingness to relieve project participants from their normal duties in a manner that neither discredits their long-term career movement nor threatens their short-term compensation. Simply advocating innovation is not enough. Senior managers must put themselves on the line if they expect their subordinates to do so.

TRANSFORMING THE IS ORGANIZATION

Middle Management Actions

Both line and IS middle managers need to take action within seven zones of activity in order to form a partnership within the environment nurtured by senior management actions.

- Educating: Implement formal and informal education programs so that superiors, peers, and subordinates can become aware of the potential benefit of applying IT to critical business tasks.
- Marketing: Plan and implement formal and informal marketing programs in order to communicate business problems and opportunities as well as new information products and services to appropriate organizational members.
- Inventing: Initiate innovative IT-related projects.
- Leading: Become a vocal and visible sponsor of IT innovation efforts.
- Compelling: Become a champion of IT innovation efforts even in the face of opposition by superiors, peers, or subordinates.
- Supporting: Provide vocal and visible endorsement of the IT-related innovation efforts of others.
- Trusting: Be willing to accept innovative IT-related projects initiated by others even when the outcome seems uncertain.

Exhibits 3-2 and 3-3 provide more detailed descriptions of these middle management actions within both domains of today's IS context.

These middle management actions include not only actions personally undertaken by a middle manager but also those programs initiated by the middle manager. As an illustration, consider the following marketing programs:

- The IS organization at Norton Company promotes its services through flyers, posters, T-shirts and gifts, a newsletter, one-on-one meetings with managers at all levels, and group presentations.[7]
- The IS organization at Owens-Corning uses line manager "champions" to sell information products and services by pitching success stories to their peers during management briefing programs. Considerable time is spent identifying appropriate "pitchmen" and selecting the right IS manager to work with each pitchman.[8]
- At Continental Bank, each member of a 17-person internal marketing group within the IS organization is assigned to a segment of the bank. Each manager then markets existing IS products and services, trains employees, and identifies new products and services.[9]

These varied programs represent concerted efforts by innovative

Exhibit 3-2. Middle Management Actions Facilitating IT Innovation in the Business Platform

Action	IS Management	Line Management
Educating	Ensure that all personnel achieve adequate levels of computing literacy	Ensure that IS personnel achieve adequate levels of knowledge of business activities
Marketing	Identify technologies most relevant for key work units and then "sell" that unit's employees on the benefits of using these technologies	Identify the work unit's critical success factors and "sell" IS personnel on the need to apply IT to these issues
Inventing	Actively search for new applications of IT across all work units	Actively search for new applications of IT within work unit
Leading	Sponsor innovative IT projects across all work units	Sponsor innovative IT projects within work unit
Compelling	Be forceful when introducing information products and services	Be forceful when undertaking IT projects
Supporting	Become an advocate of application initiatives emerging from work units	Become an advocate of technology initiatives emerging from IS
Trusting	Introduce information products and services at the request of line managers even when the outcome is uncertain	Experiment with IT at the request of IS managers even when the outcome is uncertain

IS managers to fit a marketing strategy to their organization's management style.

Partnership Mechanisms

Can an organization be transformed so that these senior and middle management actions represent an organization's norms? We contend that such a transformation occurs as an outcome of normal business interactions between the IS unit and other organizational work units.

Exhibit 3-3. Middle Management Actions Facilitating IT Innovation in the Technology Platform

Action	IS Management	Line Management
Educating	Ensure that all employees are aware of the existence and capability of the technology platform	Ensure that IS personnel are aware of work unit plans
Marketing	Identify technologies most relevant for the technology platform and make sure that line management understands the strategic impact of these technologies	Identify key work unit strategic thrusts and make sure that IS personnel are aware of these thrusts
Inventing	Actively search for new technologies that can improve or extend the technology platform	Actively search for strategic thrusts that exploit the technology platform
Leading	Sponsor innovative IT projects to enhance the technology platform	Sponsor strategic thrusts that exploit the technology platform
Compelling	Be forceful in enhancing the technology platform	Be forceful in undertaking strategic thrusts
Supporting	Become an advocate of strategic thrusts emerging from work units	Become an advocate of projects improving the technology platform
Trusting	Enhance the technology platform at the request of line managers even when the outcome is uncertain	Experiment with exploiting the technology platform at the request of IS managers even when the outcome is uncertain

These activities must be seen as the routine manner in which work is carried out and not as special efforts undertaken to achieve singular aims.

Partnership relations should thus reflect informal, rather than formal, interactions among line and IS managers. They should arise because each party involved benefits from interactions that take place. If these interactions occur because they are mandated, it is unlikely

BUILDING RELATIONSHIPS

that the senior and middle management actions described above will be pursued aggressively.

An effective but relatively unobtrusive means of influencing managerial behaviors involves the use of two types of formal organizational mechanisms:

- Structural: the people structures through which work is performed;
- Management systems: the planning and control systems that coordinate work activities and reward high performance.

To a large extent, these mechanisms define the nature of the interactions among an organization's managers. We refer to such mechanisms as *partnership mechanisms*, and they are important for three main reasons:

1. They create business relationships among line and IS managers;
2. They can signal the importance of these relationships;
3. They reinforce informal relationships once interaction has been established.

Establishing an appropriate balance between formal and informal partnership relations is not an easy task. Relying on too many formal mechanisms can break down the sense of mutual commitment so critical to effective partnership relations. Relying on too many informal mechanisms can result in partnership relations that atrophy over time as individuals move through managerial positions. Maintaining this delicate balance thus becomes a fourth senior management role.

Structural Mechanisms

The structural issue that typically arises in discussions of today's IS context involves the decision to centralize or decentralize an organization's IS activities. Regarding this issue, general agreement seems to exist on the following trends:[10]

- Information and technology policies and standards are most often handled in a centralized manner.
- Operations are being handled in a decentralized manner.
- Systems acquisition is increasingly being handled in a decentralized manner, following guidelines promulgated from the center.

Still, the decision to centralize or decentralize an organization's IS activities very much depends on a number of factors, including (a) an organization's overall posture on centralization, (b) the extent to which information products and services are linked to organizational strategies (which builds pressure for decentralization), and (c) the extent to which common data flows are critical to many, if not all, of an organization's work units (which builds pressures for centralization). Given these factors, any prescriptions here to centralize or decentralize are inappropriate, nor is it clear how centralization or decentralization of IS decision-making would, by itself, promote and sustain partnership relations between line and IS managers. Two other structural issues are, however, directly relevant to the formation of partnership relations. *Structural overlays* and *joint ventures* both span a variety of IS activities and bring line and IS managers together in carrying out these activities.

Structural Overlays

A formal organizational structure usually depicts the official assignment of managerial responsibilities throughout an organization. A structural overlay refers to arrangements of personnel that are superimposed on this official structure. These structural overlays are used most often for three purposes:

1. To bring representatives from a number of work units together to jointly handle a task that benefits from multiple interests or perspectives;
2. To handle tasks that fall outside the official responsibilities of a specific work unit;
3. To encourage behaviors not promoted through the formal assignment of work responsibilities.

Many IS activities represent situations like these, so structural overlays provide a way to form partnership relations.

Eight types of structural overlays are particularly useful in today's IS context.

- Steering committees and advisory boards bring together different perspectives and interests on a relatively permanent basis for resolving IS-related issues.
- Task forces and joint application development teams are temporary, interdisciplinary work groups formed to solve problems or to introduce new information technologies.

- Technology transfer groups are a more permanent means for introducing new information technologies.
- Liaison positions, the use of outside consultants, and career pathing represent individual rather than group means of promoting IS initiatives.

Some, if not most, of these structural overlays can be observed in most organizations. What is typically not observed is the proactive use of overlays to promote innovative behaviors. Most organizations use a lot of discretion on personnel assignments, mission statements, performance objectives, and reviews of work groups and individual roles represented by the eight types of structural overlays. But too often they fail to foster innovation through such overlays.

Steering Committees. Steering committees are the most common—and possibly the most misused—of the structural overlays applied within the IS arena. Steering committees (permanent groups of managers representing various political interests), have "approval power" over a collection of decisions or tasks. Steering committees thus set direction, tone, and policy and serve as arbitration points within an organization. Steering committees for IS have generally proven most effective when they focus on an organization's business lines or key IS architectural issues.

Two aspects of IS steering committees are particularly important. First, deciding on and delineating a steering committee's power is a critical design decision. On which issues, if any, should a steering committee have the power to say "No!", and on which should the steering committee only have the power to say "No, we have yet not gained a consensus."? Many organizations give IS steering committees far more power than is desirable. A too-powerful steering committee not only can dilute a senior IS manager's position as an equal among other senior managers, but it can usurp IS management's rightful authority over assigned responsibilities. Overusing steering committees is a symptom of a much larger problem (inadequate oversight mechanisms or a lack of confidence in a manager), and such committees should not be used in lieu of good management.

The second important consideration is that the exercise of power must always be firmly grounded in an understanding of the issues being considered. To be effective, a steering committee must be well-educated on the issues for which it has been granted approval power.

TRANSFORMING THE IS ORGANIZATION

Advisory Boards. A steering committee without the power to say "No!" is an advisory board. Advisory boards are preferable to steering committees when the objective is to influence, and be influenced by, a constituency. This distinction between steering committees and advisory boards is evident at Manufacturers Hanover Trust, where the charter of the Corporate Management Committee (a steering committee) was expanded to include assessing the firm's technological competitive position and technology planning efforts and *approving* technological policies. At the same time, the corporation established a Technology Committee (an advisory board) of senior divisional heads and senior IS directors to review strategy and policy issues, propose items for review by the Corporate Management Committee, and provide a forum for adjudicating technology issues arising between a division and corporate IS.[11] Advisory committees are effective in building awareness of key issues, obtaining views on decisions, or conveying a common understanding about decisions, and they can be a good mechanism for encouraging the formation of partnership relations.

Task Forces. A task force is a temporary work group given a well-defined mandate. Depending on the scope and importance of the mandate, task forces are formed at all organizational levels. While their narrow focus and limited life promote a task orientation that is much different from the political orientation of steering committees or advisory boards, specific partnership relations can be nurtured through personnel assignments and performance objectives.

Joint Application Development Teams. Like a task force, the joint application development team is another temporary interdisciplinary work group. Here, however, line and IS representatives are given a joint accountability to reach agreement on an information system's requirements. As practiced in a number of firms—such as IBM Canada, Avon, and Empire Blue Cross/Blue Shield—a trained JAD facilitator can usually get group consensus in a couple of days. By emphasizing the desirability and importance of line and IS cooperation, an effective JAD facilitator can build partnership relations that last long after this joint task is accomplished. The following wry statement by an IS manager at New York Life indicates what can be achieved through Joint Application Development Teams: "The success of this approach can be seen in that, for the first time, the ability to go forward on a software project may be affected by the unavail-

70

ability of users rather than the unavailability of programming resources."[12]

Technology Transfer Groups. An increasing number of IS organizations have found it worthwhile to form permanent interdisciplinary groups responsible for maintaining an awareness of, disseminating knowledge about, and managing the introduction of new information technologies. Often, such groups within IS are referred to as "advanced technology" or "R&D" groups. Perhaps the best known technology transfer group is Citicorp's Transaction Technology, Inc. (TTI), an internal think tank formed in 1971 to design and test systems using the latest in computer and communications technologies. One application in particular illustrates the important role that TTI plays within Citicorp. The biggest single factor in Citicorp's consumer banking success is the ATM, through which 80 percent of Citicorp's customers do 50 percent of their banking transactions. Citicorp began investing in ATMs a decade before many of its peers, when it created a mock bank in the basement of a New York office building to serve as a "lab" to test new products and services. By 1977, when Citicorp was ready to deploy its ATMs on a large scale, the ATM used was a sixth-generation prototype (the first five were designed, built, tested in the lab, and scrapped). Competitors admit that these 10-year-old ATMS are still better than any others on the market.[13]

Another bank with a technology transfer group is First Union in Charlotte, North Carolina, which formed a special projects group that sits between its IS organization and its operating divisions. This group is staffed solely by project managers, each of whom set up and then manage interdisciplinary teams investigating new information products and services for all segments of the bank. The corporate IS organization at Air Products and Chemicals calls its technology transfer group the Emerging Technologies Department which handles, among other things, technology assessment and technology R&D as well as both technology and knowledge transfer.[14]

Technology transfer can fail without such support. For example, the many technologies developed at Xerox's Palo Alto Research Center but not introduced into Xerox's operations can be traced directly to the absence of technology transfer groups. If line and IS managers are not brought together, it is unlikely that true technology transfer will occur.

Liaison Positions. It is possible to overlay an organization's formal structure at the individual as well as the group level. Liaison positions, e.g., having an individual serve as a liaison between the IS organization and another work unit, are the most common example of an "individual overlay."

Liaison roles may be staffed by either IS personnel or by line personnel. For example:

- Line managers at Frito-Lay serve as "functional interface managers" for each line unit where their main focus is to integrate information products and services with their unit's marketing strategy.
- Support groups of users within each line unit are being created at American Industries and Metropolitan Life.[15]
- Each of the five business units at the Royal Bank of Canada has a system architect, system administrator, and a system account executive, all of whom report to business unit management.
- IS technology specialists at Union Carbide are being placed in line units, where they then report to line management.[16]
- IS personnel within the Customer Automation Support group at Hartford Life are posted to line units to serve as a single point-of-contact.[17]
- IS "account executives" who know where to go within the IS organization to make things happen at Houston Power & Light are assigned to one or more line units so that each line unit has a single point of contact within the IS organization.[18]
- Senior IS executives at Cigna Corporation are assigned to each of Cigna's business units to manage the relations between the IS organization and the unit.[19]

Liaison positions serve as a vehicle through which otherwise absent knowledge, perspectives, and values can be embedded within both line and IS units. Thus, they can play a key role in forging partnership relations between line and IS managers.

Consultants. A second type of individual overlay is the use of outside consultants to introduce fresh perspectives or upgrade the level of expertise available for a task. Consultants can serve three major roles:

1. To contribute an action plan;
2. To provide a second opinion on an action plan;
3. To implement the action plan.

While much can be gained from the use of outsiders in bolstering partnership relations among line and IS managers, by themselves they do little to establish relations. Thus, care must be taken that consultants are used to establish or augment, and not replace, partnership relations.

Career Pathing. A third type of individual overlay involves carefully managing the career paths of an organization's managers and professionals so that individuals move through a succession of job assignments within both the IS and line organizations. This movement provides individuals with a knowledge of both of the work domains of IS and it equips managers throughout the organization with extensive partnership networks.

Joint Ventures

The high levels of funding and uncertainty associated with many IS projects inhibit innovative activities. To overcome this problem, the IS unit can enter a joint venture with one or more of its organization's work groups to develop and implement an information product or service. This is an example of a true partnership, where each party bears risk and shares in the benefits of a successful project.

Joint ventures most often arise in one of two ways. First, one or more line units desire either to acquire knowledge, to acquire a new technology, or to implement an application but cannot justify the required funding. Through joint funding with the IS unit, line units are able to attain their objective and IS builds good will and credibility. Second, the IS unit convinces a single line unit to sponsor the development of an application with organization-wide potential. After jointly funding the application's development, the IS organization and the sponsoring line unit share in any revenues produced by "selling" the application to the organization's other line units.

Management Systems

Organizations implement planning and control systems for many reasons. One important reason is that managers can take as given those aspects of the work environment embodied in a planning or control mechanism. As a consequence, managers are then able to focus their attention on other specific issues or activities. If this were not the case, the complexities of organizational life would overwhelm most managers.

TRANSFORMING THE IS ORGANIZATION

Planning and control systems reflect their designers' preferences regarding work behaviors and outcomes as well as their designers' assumptions about the organization and its environment. To a certain extent, these preferences and assumptions can influence the actions taken by an organization's managers. Particular behaviors, such as innovation and the forming of partnership relations, can be promoted—or discouraged—through planning and control systems.

Planning Mechanisms

Because of the long lead times associated with many IT projects and the increasingly tight links between business strategic planning and IS planning, the planning activity with the greatest potential for building partnership relations between line and IS managers is long-range (3-5 years) planning. Three types of IS long-range planning activities are observed in most organizations.

- Strategic planning: Examinations of the manner in which IT can influence a business's competitive position in its various markets. This activity must be closely integrated with the business strategic planning process if it is to be successful. The output of the planning process is a time-phased statement of the information products and services and the IT resources necessary to gain market advantages.
- Systems planning: Examinations of how the organization uses information products and services in all of its managerial and work systems, and the interdependence of the products and services. This activity must be accomplished by individuals knowledgeable about how work is accomplished within the organization. The output of this planning process is a time-phased inventory of both existing and planned information systems as well as those under development.
- Technology planning: Examinations of the technology platform with outputs of the strategic and systems planning processes as givens. This planning process must anticipate to some extent likely additions to the strategic and systems plans so that technology platform constraints do not arise to limit otherwise appropriate IS plans. The output of this planning process is an inventory of the current technology platform as well as a time-phased statement of its evolution.

Each of these long-range planning processes normally has an annual planning component, directly linked with the organization's budgeting and capital appropriation cycle.

The critical question that should arise regarding planning is: "What type of planning processes should be implemented to promote and maintain partnership relations between line and IS managers?"

Success lies in developing a climate in which both line and IS managers can make a commitment to contribute to and validate these plans. All three planning processes require input from both line and IS managers. Still, each planning process must be the responsibility of either line or IS management, not both. Success seems to occur most often where line management is given the responsibility for strategic and systems planning and IS management is given the responsibility for technology planning. Success with all three planning processes, however, requires the active participation of managers from both work domains.

Two examples illustrate the nature of the processes that can evolve through well-designed IS planning systems. One is the planning procedures at Continental Bank which prompt a productive series of interactions between line and IS managers:[20] "Each of the bank's 60 business units prepares a long-range plan which is updated annually and completely reworked every few years. In one section of the plan, the business unit's major IS needs and issues must be described. The IS organization must then prepare a corporate-wide response plan in which it covers the needs and issues raised in the long-range plans developed by each business unit."

A second example is the list of benefits Pfizer, Inc. obtains from its IS planning efforts. The benefits suggest the many ways an effective planning process can build an organizational climate promoting the formation of partnership relations:[21]

- A means of eliciting viewpoints from others;
- A means of recording assumptions and priorities, and of airing new issues;
- A way of communicating IS management's vision;
- A statement of IS management's commitment to manage change within IS;
- A vehicle for securing the cooperation and commitment of line managers;
- An agenda for monthly meetings;
- A framework for day-to-day decisions.

Although in most multidivisional organizations the three planning mechanisms occur within each division and for the organization as a whole, IS management is additionally responsible for assuring that divisional IS plans are consistent with organization-wide IS plans. If an organization's divisions are highly differentiated, the divisional plans are likely to drive the entire planning process. In organizations where the divisions are tightly interconnected through material, customer, and information flows, the organization-wide plans are more likely to drive the entire planning process.

Control Mechanisms

Four managerial control issues are particularly relevant to the IS context: capital investment policies, internal pricing systems, service level agreements, and incentive schemes. Not only do these control issues generate continuing debates both among IS managers and between line and IS managers, but the manner in which each is handled can have a significant impact on the development of partnership relations between line and IS managers. Rather than discussing these control mechanisms in detail, let us examine how each can promote or inhibit the formation of partnership relations.

Capital Investment Policies. Many observers believe that the capital investment policies used by many organizations severely inhibit the ability of these organizations to introduce needed information products and services. This occurs because the payback, return-on-investment, and net present value methodologies appropriate to many other investment decisions are simply not appropriate for IT investments.

- The benefits associated with many IT investments are difficult to calculate because of the intangibility of benefits and an organization's lack of experience with a specific technology.
- The benefit streams from many IT investments are often characterized by low returns early in an application's life but high returns later.
- Many IT projects, such as those associated with database management systems and departmental systems, are difficult to justify individually but provide significant collective benefits.
- Many IT investments, particularly those associated with the technology platform, do not provide direct benefits.

Use of these traditional investment tools thus generally favors the adoption of conservative, rather than innovative, IS projects.

A further consequence of applying traditional investment tools finds a project's champions and sponsors distorting the project's costs and benefits in order to push the project through the capital appropriation process. Because distortion ultimately produces false expectations and mistrust, such behavior inhibits rather than promotes partnerships.

Alternative approaches for handling IT-related investment decisions, however, can facilitate the formation of partnership relations. Examples of such approaches include:

- Strategic discounts: Eliminating any barrier to strategic investments or having strategic projects compete against each other but not against other projects.
- Value analysis: Initially funding low-cost prototypes in order to better understand a project's costs and benefits.
- Portfolio approaches: Packaging projects together so that their different risk levels and benefit streams can be evaluated as a complete portfolio.
- Intuitive basis: Pulling projects completely out of the capital appropriation process and relying on managerial intuition and conviction.

Each of the above techniques, when correctly applied, actually requires a more comprehensive, robust assessment than do most traditional investment tools. This feature makes them particularly useful in the formation of partnership relations—line and IS managers must work together closely to build a convincing business case.

Perhaps the easiest way to circumvent an organization's existing capital investment procedures is to establish separate investment funds for innovative IT projects. (Two organizations that provide such pools of discretionary corporate funding are British Petroleum and CIBA-GEIGY.) Even with separate funding, it is important to recognize that financial resources are only part of a larger problem, because finding talented individuals to manage and implement these projects is often more difficult than obtaining the financial resources.

Internal Pricing Systems. An IS internal pricing system is instituted for three major reasons:

1. To recover the costs associated with providing information products and services;
2. To provide an equitable set of charges for information products and services;
3. To influence managerial decisions regarding the use of information products and services.

Typically, the first reason tends to dominate the designs of most IS internal pricing systems. Because of the characteristics of many in-

TRANSFORMING THE IS ORGANIZATION

formation products and services, disagreement and misunderstanding often arise with cost-recovery charges. An IS pricing system driven by a cost-recovery motive can thus split line and IS managers apart rather than pull them together.

Because the purpose of an IS internal pricing system lies more with communicating the relative values rather than actual costs of information products and services, a system driven by numbers 2 and 3 above is more likely to promote the formation of partnership relations. Arriving at and renegotiating charges within such a pricing system requires frequent and open discussions by line and IS managers on the value and accessibility of information products and services as well as their costs. The pricing system thus is an important educational and marketing linkage among line and IS managers and it serves as a fairly neutral negotiating arena.

Service Level Agreements. The concept of a service level agreement is deceptively simple: line and IS managers negotiate a formal contract that unambiguously specifies (a) IS product and service performance levels; and (b) the charges to be levied when these performance levels are attained and when they are not. Effectively handled, this negotiation process can achieve a mutuality of expectation and commitment.

At Security Pacific, service level agreements have been negotiated for all information products and services, with the standards for these agreements being business-based, not technology-based.[22] In arriving at these standards, IS management at Security Pacific asked line managers questions such as

- What is your customer interested in?
- What hurts your customer in terms of dollars or the way you do business?
- What can we measure to prove that we are doing a good job in helping you serve your customers?

As with internal pricing systems, a well-designed service level agreement program can serve as a valuable communications and negotiation device among line and IS managers.

Incentive Schemes. Finally an organization's incentive schemes can provide an organizational climate that induces line and IS managers to forge partnership relations. Regardless of whether the incentives are financial (bonuses, stock options, commissions, etc.) or career-oriented (knowledge, skills, and experience), the intent should be to tightly link individual and work unit rewards to business success. As mentioned earlier, partnership relations only work when all parties believe it is in their individual interests to work together toward a common objective.

Incentives such as discretionary bonuses and stock options, which have historically been limited to senior executives, are now generally creeping lower in organizations—even in IS organizations. For example:

- At Security Pacific, annual bonuses are being given to IS managers who achieve their service level agreements.[23]
- The National Institutes of Health are awarding bonuses to those IS personnel who achieve agreed-on "sales" targets in delivering products and services to users.
- Alamo Rent A Car has developed incentive plans for programmers (developing an application reliably and on time can earn a programming team up to $25,000) and operators (operators share in a bonus pool which is credited 10 cents for every minute of uptime where average response time is less than one second but debited $10 for every minute of downtime).[24]

The key to effectiveness is to tie such plans to quantifiable objectives that clearly benefit the organization and are under the control of the individuals involved.

Conclusion

All of an organization's managers—both line and IS—are responsible for promoting the innovative uses of information products and services. This discussion recommends courses of action for senior and middle managers, and emphasizes the importance of building partnership relations among line managers and IS managers. It also identifies a number of mechanisms to promote the formation of these partnership relations.

Managers who desire to reorient their organization's climate so that it is conducive to innovation can take three actions:

1. Leverage the managerial tools in current use.
    - Do they promote or inhibit risk-taking by line and IS managers?

TRANSFORMING THE IS ORGANIZATION

- Do they encourage or discourage risk-sharing between line and IS managers?
- Do they tend to produce mutual understanding or conflict among line and IS managers?

Over time, an organization's structure and its management systems will determine the behaviors of its members.

2. Leverage the initiative of middle management.
    - Do middle managers personally engage in or avoid innovative behaviors?
    - Do they encourage or discourage the innovative behaviors of others?
    - Are they knowledgeable or ignorant of the links among IT, the organization's business activities, and the competitive marketplace?
    - Do they see value or danger in entering into arrangements where they must in part depend on others in order to achieve business success?

Middle managers play such a critical role in applying IT that a single weak link in the managerial chain can effectively deter an organization's ability to maintain its position in the marketplace.

3. Leverage the values and behaviors of senior management.
    - Do senior managers agree or disagree about the importance of IT in the organization's ability to compete in the marketplace?
    - Do they agree or disagree about the role that technology leadership plays in business strategies?
    - Do they agree or disagree about the desirability and rate of organizational innovation?

The values of the senior management team will inevitably influence the directions in which the organization moves.

The first and most important step in an extended effort to turn an organization around is recognizing the need to make changes in an organization's structure, its management systems, and in the values and behaviors of its middle and senior managers. The arguments and issues raised in this chapter should be useful in convincing others of the need to change as well as in determining the direction of that change.

Notes

1. Zmud, R.W., A.C. Boynton, and G.C. Jacobs. "The Information Economy: A New Perspective for Effective Information Systems Management," *Data Base*, Fall 1986, pp. 5–16.
2. Souder, W.E. *Management Decision Methods for Managers of Engineering and Research*, Van Nostrand Reinhold Company, New York, 1980.
3. See note 1.
4. Norton, R.E. "Citibank Wows the Consumer," *Fortune*, June 8, 1987, pp. 49–54.
5. Carlyle, R.E. "Color Me Blue," *Datamation*, January 1, 1987, pp. 85–86.
6. Galbraith, J.R. "Designing the Innovating Organization," *Organizational Dynamics*, Winter 1982, pp. 5–25.
7. Ludlum, D.A. "Norton Markets its MIS," *Computerworld*, November 24, 1986, pp. 63 and 68.
8. *SIM Network*, "Member Profile," Oct./Nov. 1986, pp. 6, 7, 10, and 11.
9. Harvard Business School, "Continental Bank," HBS Case 9-183-044, Boston, Mass., 1983.
10. See note 1.
11. La Belle, A., and H.E. Nyce. "Whither the IT Organization?," *Sloan Management Review*, Summer 1987, pp. 75–85.
12. *Computerworld*. "MIS Today: Managing to Competitive Advantage," June 16, 1986, pp. 57–72.
13. See note 4.
14. Harvard Business School. "Air Products and Chemicals, Inc. (C): The Emerging Technologies Department," HBS Case 9-185-015, Boston, Mass., 1985.
15. Radding A. "All Action, No Talk?," *Computerworld*, May 18, 1987, pp. 81–87.
16. See note 15.
17. See note 15.
18. *PC Week*. "Houston Power & Light Demands High Wattage from its PCs," April 28, 1987, pp. 53 and 56.
19. Williamson, M. "Taking Care of Business," *Computerworld*, June 1, 1987, pp. 20th/30 and 20th/31.
20. See note 9.
21. Cassese, V., W. Gruber, and M. Hughes. "Planning Amid Change," *Computerworld*, December 9, 1985, pp. 71–75.

TRANSFORMING THE IS ORGANIZATION

22. *Computerworld.* "Interview—John Singleton: He Makes a Profit out of DP," February 10, 1987, pp. 58, 64–66.
23. See note 22.
24. Connolly, J. "Incentives Drive Alamo's MIS," *Computerworld*, April 27, 1987, pp. 71 and 74.

CHAPTER FOUR

ESTABLISHING COOPERATIVE EXTERNAL RELATIONSHIPS

JOYCE J. ELAM

The highly centralized IS organization of the past is evolving into a decentralized, streamlined, and value-added organization. Three converging forces drive this evolution.

The first force is the growing importance of information technology to organizations. The use of information technology to achieve competitive advantage has caught the attention of senior management and information technology is becoming, in many organizations, absolutely central to the implementation of strategic initiatives. In others, information technology is becoming a critical component of the products and services they offer. As businesses become increasingly information intensive, information technology will be the mechanism differentiating the successful from the not-successful. This new heightened visibility and importance of information technology puts pressure on the traditional IS organization to deliver a distinctively different class of applications. The IS organization will find itself in need of an expanded knowledge base of new concepts and technologies if it is going to be able to deliver such applications.

The second force in the evolution toward decentralization is technology itself. Now it is possible for end users within organizations—and specialized software vendors outside organizations—to provide services that are more reliable, more functional, and less expensive than those developed in-house by IS professionals. This force is asserting itself as organizations strive to streamline in highly competitive environments and scramble to find ways to improve performance.

The third force is the shortage of IS professionals, particularly those with highly specialized technical knowledge. All indications are that fewer graduates plan to become computer programmers

TRANSFORMING THE IS ORGANIZATION

and systems analysts. (For example, a recent survey completed by the University of California at Los Angeles and the American Council on Education found that only 3 percent of college freshman were interested in careers as computer programmers or systems analysts. This is down from 8 percent in 1982.) Many IS organizations report great difficulties in obtaining and keeping a fully staffed IS organization, with turnover rates frequently exceeding 10 percent. Much of the experience of IS veterans is being invalidated by requirements to function in the new environment that is emerging. Technical experts in such fields as Artificial Intelligence (AI) remain scarce and expensive.

As a result of these three forces, internal resources and capabilities may not conform with what the IS organization is being asked to accomplish. Too few resources and capabilities may be available to build the strategic, competitive systems and too many resources and capabilities may be available for back office applications that can be performed more economically outside.

Tremendous pressure is being placed on the IS organization to change. The traditional role of IS as the place where all information processing activities occur is fast disappearing, as evidenced by the increasing movement of application development out of the IS organization to end users in line organizations. As the responsibilities for information processing activities expand past the boundaries of the traditional IS organization, the IS organization of tomorrow will be faced with a new and important challenge—that of developing, managing, and coordinating cooperative arrangements between itself and other external parties both within the organization and beyond.

The purpose of this chapter is to provide guidance to senior IS executives on how to meet this challenge, particularly with respect to those cooperative arrangements that extend beyond the firm's boundary. A framework drawn from transaction cost theory will be presented as an aid in identifying those information processing activities that should remain the responsibility of the central IS organization and those for which the responsibilities should be shared with other parties. Two different strategies for establishing external cooperative arrangements—one of divestiture and one of acquisition—will then be described and illustrated through a set of mini-cases. The chapter will close by listing a set of guidelines for senior IS executives to consider when developing external cooperative relationships.

Markets and Hierarchies: A Framework for Viewing the IS Organization

A transaction is an exchange of goods or services between two entities. Transaction costs are the costs to conduct a transaction over and above the production costs of the goods or services exchanged, and they include the costs of negotiating and monitoring the contract on which the transaction is based. Transaction cost theory focuses on determining the appropriate "governance structure" for each transaction. To govern transactions involving the flow of materials or services within and through the value chain (i.e., the collection of activities that are performed to design, produce, market, deliver, and support its products and services), organizations use two basic mechanisms: markets and hierarchies.[1]

Whenever an organization chooses to purchase goods and services rather than produce them itself, the organization is engaged in transactions governed by market mechanisms. A printing company that does not own printing presses or a clothing retailer that does not own manufacturing facilities must engage in market transactions to obtain the production capacity needed to deliver products to its customers. The terms of the transaction—such as price, quality, and quantity—are determined by the forces of supply and demand.

Whenever an organization controls and directs activities through some type of predefined management structure for a single administrative entity (e.g., the firm, a division, etc.), the organization is engaged in transactions governed by a hierarchy. The insurance company whose salesmen are employees rather than independent agents or the fruit distributor that owns its own orchards engages in transactions governed by management decisions and policies rather than by market forces.

Factors Favoring Markets or Hierarchies

Transaction cost theory identifies two costs to be considered in determining whether the appropriate governance structure for a transaction is a market or a hierarchy: production costs and transactions costs. Production costs tend to be lower for markets due to the fact that competition makes products and services available in the market at efficient prices. Transaction costs tend to be lower for hierarchies since coordination activities are handled through established policies that eliminate the need to gather and analyze a great deal of information.

In evaluating the appropriate governance structure for transactions involving information processing activities, one additional factor must be considered. This factor involves organizational learning. In a pure market, transactions between two parties occur at arm's length. Very little occurs in the way of sharing information, technology, or skills. When organizational learning is important, a hierarchical structure provides a much superior environment for facilitating it.

A Market Approach for Meeting Information Processing Requirements

The framework of markets and hierarchies can help interpret many of the predictions being made about the future of IS organizations. One of these predictions is the demise of the in-house IS organization.[2] This view contends that the activities provided by today's IS department through an internal hierarchical structure can be provided at far lower cost and at far higher quality through market transactions involving independent organizations. In some cases one of these independent organizations will be an independent subsidiary, formed from the specialized IS base within the company. However, as far as the organization is concerned, dealing with this subsidiary is no different from dealing with an independent supplier. Interpreted from the perspective of markets and hierarchies, this view assumes that the reduced production costs realized by implementing market transactions for all information processing activities outweigh the increased coordination costs incurred. The recent trend toward turning IS departments into profit centers is seen as the first step toward this scenario.[3] The movement towards market transactions for information processing activities is echoed in other scenarios for the IS organization of tomorrow. In a scenario proposed by J. Rockart and M. Treacy,[4] line management takes charge of conceiving and implementing the organization's systems. The IS organization maintains the systems, operates the technical infrastructure, and educates line management about technology. Information processing activities thus become distributed throughout the organization.

Both of these views foresee a reduction in the production activities of IS organizations due to the reduced production costs of performing these activities elsewhere. Future IS organizations are either non-

ESTABLISHING COOPERATIVE EXTERNAL RELATIONSHIPS

existent or have responsibility for merely a subset of their former activities. The arguments for both of these views hinge on looking at the reduction in production costs. However, neither view explicitly considers transaction costs or opportunity costs for organizational learning.

What these views fail to recognize is that as the IS organization loses many responsibilities associated with production activities, it gains others associated with coordination activities. The need to facilitate organizational learning will demand that IS continue to play a role in production activities even though, from a purely economic perspective, all production activities could be handled outside the IS organization. It is therefore unlikely that the IS organization will go away as Dearden predicts or that the IS organization of tomorrow will be a strict subset of the IS organization of today as Rockart and Treacy predict. What is more likely is that the IS organization will become more and more involved with market transactions and increased coordination responsibilities as the performance of traditional IS activities is dispersed outside its boundaries.

The view of the IS organization of tomorrow that emerges from this discussion is a centralized IS organization that maintains a set of cooperative arrangements with external parties and that functions in a coordinating role: assigning responsibility for performance of work while accounting for production, coordination, and opportunity costs for organizational learning.

How will this new IS organization use cooperative relationships to develop, maintain, and operate the strategic systems and the back office systems for which it retains clear responsibility? The following two propositions concern the use of cooperative arrangements in the future IS organization:

1. In developing back office and factory applications, the IS organization will seek cooperative arrangements (external to the organization) that result in the divestment of skills, knowledge, and technology.
2. In developing strategic applications, the IS organization will seek cooperative arrangements (external to the organization) that result in the acquisition of new skills, knowledge, and technology.

Following is a general overview of cooperative arrangements describing the benefits usually associated with such arrangements. The two sections that follow support the propositions above.

Cooperative Arrangements

The material in this section, which reviews cooperative arrangements at the macro level, is drawn from an excellent book on this subject.[5]

Cooperative arrangements fall into three main categories: (a) full-equity ownership; (b) partial ownership, and (c) no ownership control.

Arrangements involving full-equity ownership include mergers and acquisitions and internal venturing. In the case of mergers and acquisitions, organizations recognize the need for external resources and skills. Because they want full control over how these resources and skills are employed, they attempt to turn market transactions into hierarchical transactions. Internal venturing also assumes that management wants more control than would normally be possible with an outside organization. This arrangement will be pursued if the dominant culture of the firm makes it difficult for innovative ideas to surface and flourish. Through an internal venture, the firm hopes that supporting entrepreneurial ideas and keeping the venture outside the mainstream of business will produce a steady stream of innovations.

Arrangements involving partial ownership include joint ventures and minority investments. A joint venture is a separate entity with two or more firms as partners and with its own assets and management team. Through a joint venture, it is hoped that synergies will arise from the strengths of each partner and create a superior competitor. Minority investments involve the purchase of equity in an established firm rather than the establishment of a separate entity. Gaining access to technology, skills, and specialized knowledge important to the accomplishment of strategic objectives is a primary reason for such investments.

Cooperative arrangements involving no ownership control include cooperative agreements, research and development partnerships, and cross-licensing and cross-distribution agreements. Cooperative agreements are based on contracts rather than equity. Research and development partnerships are agreements to fund research. These partnerships involve a research consortium of several firms in a particular industry with the goal of accelerating the industry's rate of innovation through technical cooperation. Cross-licensing agreements allow a firm to gain knowledge about processes that another firm has developed. Cross-distribution arrangements permit one firm to market the products of another in a specified geographic region.

Three major motivations drive managers to consider cooperative arrangements even though such arrangements are administratively much more complex than acting alone: internal benefits, competitive benefits, and strategic benefits. The internal benefits that are derived from cooperative arrangements include sharing costs and risks; obtaining financing; sharing facilities that benefit from economies of scale; obtaining information on new technologies and new customers; and identifying innovative managerial practices. The competitive benefits include influencing the industry structure's evolution, preempting competition, presenting a defensive response to blurring industry boundaries and globalization, and creating more effective competitors. Finally, strategic benefits include the creation and exploitation of synergies, the transfer of technology and skills, and diversification.

Establishing Cooperative Arrangements for Back Office and Support Applications

Applications that fall into the category of back office or support applications have the following common characteristics:

1. They are well-defined and repetitive;
2. They involve common business functions;
3. While they are critical to the ongoing operations of the business, they do not represent the high-value applications that will enhance the competitive positioning of the organization.

In many ways these applications can be considered a commodity, and as such the IS organization realizes little value in owning and maintaining it.

Firms that specialize in developing systems for particular applications (such as payroll, compilers, defense) often produce far more computer code at less cost, in less time, and with higher performance simply because they have become subject-matter experts in their specialty area. As an IS organization reaches its limit on the complexity of work and the amount of attention it can devote to performing its work, establishing a cooperative arrangement where an external party has responsibility for back office and support applications frees up internal resources for use on high-value applications.

Cooperative arrangements like this allow an organization to divest itself of certain skills, knowledge, and responsibilities. Companies have both economic and technical incentives to divest themselves of such

TRANSFORMING THE IS ORGANIZATION

internal IS functions in order to remain competitive and control production costs.

If the entire application portfolio of an IS department is composed of back office and support applications, a case can be made for an organization to totally divest itself of the IS function. Because these applications are widely understood and available from other sources, coordination costs of defining requirements, negotiating prices, etc. should be relatively small.

The most effective cooperative arrangement for back office and support applications is one that minimizes the organization's involvement and use of its resources. This is because organizational learning and information sharing is not important. The IS organization and the external party in the cooperative arrangement deal at arm's length with each other and the motivations for the cooperative arrangement are primarily internal, that is, they allow certain tasks to be performed more efficiently in an external party's facility. Some examples of the types of cooperative arrangements for back office and support applications follow.

Full-Equity Ownership

The centralized IS group of British Leyland had provided outside commercial data processing services since the late 1970s.

The IS group had a history of being innovative. It successfully installed the first private microwave data communications network in the United Kingdom and developed important CAD/CAM applications. The IS group also provided outside commercial data processing services. Starting with electronic mail, the group built its outside processing to 20 percent of its business. Eventually, the IS group was set up as a wholly owned subsidiary and British Leyland contracted with this subsidiary to provide data processing services.

British Leyland, however, kept what it saw as its strategic systems, the CAD/CAM applications, for example. Each British Leyland plant was responsible for its own information processing requirements and a small centralized group coordinated these activities. Subsequently the subsidiary was sold but a close working relationship with British Leyland was maintained. When British Leyland itself was sold and the company became the Austin Rover Group, maintaining a long-term contract with the subsidiary was part of the agreement. Another example of a cooperative arrangement involving full-equity ownership is the widespread use of overseas software facilities by U.S. computer vendors for operations and data entry. This practice is now expanding to include software design, development, testing, and maintenance.[6] For example, Travelers Corporation recently joined a small number of U.S. corporations in setting up a subsidiary in Ireland for design, development, and testing of its application software. The chief advantage of the Irish site is the work force, which is well educated, loyal, and less expensive than in the U.S. American Airlines has also looked into locating a software development facility in Ireland and in India. Last July, Geisco, the division of General Electric Company that provides network-based services such as remote processing and electronic data interchange, opened a software development facility in Dublin.

This development of software facilities by a number of U.S. computer and software vendors—including IBM, Digital Equipment Corporation, Wang Corporation, and Lotus Development Corporation—can be attributed to Ireland's Industrial Development Authority. The cost of hiring software professionals in Ireland is about 60 percent of doing so in Massachusetts and the overall cost of operating a software facility in Ireland is about half that in the United States.

No Ownership Control

"Cycle-sharing" is an example of an emerging cooperative arrangement with no ownership. In cycle-sharing, organizations cooperate with divisions, subsidiaries, or external parties to take advantage of differences in peak-load hours to distribute their processing needs to sites that would otherwise sit idle. For example, the IS director for a large multinational bank is currently exploring opportunities for cycle-sharing with other subsidiaries that are operating in different time zones. A French-based multinational parent corporation, GSI, has implemented a procedure to take advantage of its different peak-load demands at geographically dispersed divisions.

A well-established type of cooperative arrangement involving no ownership is contract programming and design services.[7] It is estimated that the market for contract programming and design services will double to $10.4 billion by 1990, primarily as a result of a shortage of data processing professionals. Much of the growth in demand for software consulting services can be attributed to the recent moves by software services firms to offer more full-service consulting involving the design and complete development of a system.

It should be noted that the use of outside consulting services is a concern to some IS directors. Consultants are expensive and the experience they gain is not captured by the organization. Contract programmers can cause resentment among permanent workers. The issue of expense is debatable, but losing expertise and possibly creating resentments are real concerns. For these reasons, this type of cooperative arrangement should only be used for back office and support applications where expertise is not an issue and where the internal staff is devoted to working on the higher value, strategic applications.

Another type of no-ownership arrangement is that of remote computing services (RCS), which are positioning themselves to serve data processing departments as dedicated "IS shadows".[8] The RCS vendors say they can serve as potent IS allies, providing standardized business computing systems in areas such as marketing support for distribution and sales or production management. Agreements with RCS vendors also provide IS departments with new technologies such as electronic mail, micro-to-mainframe links, and electronically developed software. Several vendors even use the term *cooperative processing* when referring to their new relationships with IS. In deciding whether to use an RCS the key question is "can the RCS offer reliable services more cost effectively than IS?" Frequently, the answer to this question is "yes" for back office and support applications.

RCS can contribute expertise in financial applications. Many RCS have years of experience performing corporate payroll, cash flow, inventory, and order-entry functions. Firms that establish cooperative arrangements with RCS can control costs, use proven systems that can be quickly implemented, and minimize their involvement in recruiting IS professionals in a highly competitive marketplace.

Establishing Cooperative Arrangements for Strategic Applications

Some IS organizations have begun to consider cooperative arrangements for strategic systems because they do not have the in-house expertise to develop such systems and the costs (primarily of production) of developing this expertise from scratch are prohibitively high. IS organizations of tomorrow cannot hope to develop in-house the many technologies they need and they cannot afford to fund all of the projects that help the organization remain competitive on several fronts.

Cooperative arrangements are the only answer to this dilemma.

ESTABLISHING COOPERATIVE EXTERNAL RELATIONSHIPS

Economic considerations favor a market method, but because enhancing organizational learning is a primary goal for strategic systems, any cooperative arrangements must allow the organization to "acquire" knowledge and skill that can be transferred in-house. Thus, cooperative arrangements that involve a close working relationship between the IS organization and the external party should be pursued. Such a working relationship will involve some measure of hierarchical control.

As mentioned before, motivations for establishing cooperative arrangements are internal (particularly obtaining information on new technologies and identifying innovative managerial practices); competitive (particularly in providing both offensive and defensive responses to competitive challenges); and strategic (particularly in creating synergies and transferring technology and skills). Following are some examples of cooperative arrangements for strategic applications.

Full-Equity Ownership

Cooperative arrangements involving full-equity ownership are occurring between large multinational organizations and leading technology firms. One such arrangement exists between GSI, a French-based multinational parent corporation, and Transcomm Data Systems (TDS) based in Pittsburgh, Pennsylvania, and Syntelligence, located in Sunnyvale, California. Both of these artificial-intelligence technology firms market packaged expert systems. The motivations for such arrangements are strategic — they allow a large organization like GSI to gain expertise in areas where it previously did not compete, especially if it is attempting to provide a vertically integrated product base.

Sometimes, organizations enter into these arrangements as a result of a failed cooperative arrangement with no ownership control. A cooperative arrangement between a large health services organization that delivered health care products through retail outlets and a small leading-edge technology firm in an enterprise called the Retail Automation Project ended this way. The IS director at the health services organization initiated a project to install microcomputers in all retail stores around the United States. In order to keep the expense of supplying each store with a microcomputer at a reasonable level, he contracted with a technology firm to assemble customized microcomputers for the stores. The technology firm was greatly undercapitalized and eventually was unable to deliver on the contract. The health services organization subsequently bought the firm and now has a separate internal group responsible for the Retail Automation Project, including the manufacturing of microcomputers.

A major international bank has set up an independent subsidiary whose charter will be to pursue innovative projects. This subsidiary will be a holding company for any number of independent ventures surrounding the development of products for a particular technology such as the support of electronic data interchange (EDI) between banks. Such an organization is not constrained by existing practices and allows the IS group within the bank to pursue activities that would be difficult to pursue otherwise.

Partial Ownership

A good example of a joint venture involving partial ownership is a major international bank whose IS director has created a division called Technology Ventures. The charter for this new division is to identify opportunities for developing new products through joint ventures with external parties, and to set up and participate in the management of the joint ventures. Two possible joint ventures have been identified: (a) with a large software company to develop a set of common delivery modules that allow users' terminals to interface with host computers, and (b) with a small leading-edge technology firm to develop an on-line training and reference guide for bank employees. Each of these are seen as joint ventures because each organization will equally contribute capital and equally share in the benefits.

Another interesting example involves a number of rival Wall Street investment banking firms. These firms are considering a joint venture to purchase a local area communication network for the banking firms in the Wall Street area so that they can process trading and pricing information more efficiently. Costs of individual ownership are prohibitive, as are the extremely high costs charged by current vendors, so these firms are negotiating to distribute the expenses and the operating costs among members of the consortium. Such a joint venture is interesting because it redefines the relationships of traditional competitors and identifies opportunities for cooperation. This example is considered a strategic application because it involves defining a technical infrastructure upon which other applications are based.

Large multinational organizations are buying minority stakes in small venture-backed businesses in order for the IS group to get a relatively inexpensive peek at new technologies, products, and markets. The cooperative arrangement also provides the organization with access to specialized skills and knowledge that can be transferred into the primary organization for use on its own development projects. One such cooperative arrangement exists between Metaphor, an organization that markets a professional productivity system, and TEKNOWLEDGE, an organization in the AI field, and a large consumer products organization.

No Ownership: Joint Applications Development

An example of joint applications development is a major service organization faced with an immediate need to replace a set of 11 independent, outdated order entry systems. Its objective was a single, consolidated order entry and billing system. It was estimated that the development of such a project using internal resources would require more than 400 people, 30 months to complete, and more than $100 million. These requirements were unacceptable to both senior IS and line management so the IS organization decided to use a cooperative arrangement as a way of getting the new system on-line more quickly; it entered a contractual agreement with a small software company that developed its own design technique along with a COBOL applications generator.

The software company took on the role of project manager. Ten employees of the service organization who were included in the project development team physically relocated to the site of the contractor. The task of the contractor was to educate the project team in the new design technique and then to oversee the use of this technique in designing and programming the system. The contractor developed the pilot system in three months, and the entire project will probably be completed in nine months at a cost of under $10 million. Although this cooperative arrangement was considered the only way to get the job done, an equally important goal was to facilitate organizational learning of a new innovative design technique. The challenge now is to establish cooperative arrangements with the contractor to facilitate this transfer of knowledge.

Another example of a cooperative arrangement involving a joint application development project involves Ford and IBM.[9] Ford and IBM recently entered a $200 million cooperative arrangement to develop an integrated office system that would allow the use of a variety of equipment. A team of 50 Ford and IBM executives is designing the system to fit Ford's needs and it is jointly overseeing installation. In establishing this cooperative arrangement, IBM was forced to abandon its sales approach of the past decade. "[Ford] asked to start with a blank piece of paper and redefine how the relationship between the two companies should work," says William W.K. Rich, an IBM assistant group executive, "so we did." As part of this new relationship, IBM is lifting its usual shroud of secrecy about future products. It has provided Ford with confidential information so that Ford can take advantage of any planned, but unannounced, products in designing its new office system.

As a final example, Syntelligence is currently engaged with IBM in a cross-licensing cooperative arrangement on the IMAP (Industry Manufacturing Automation Protocol). Syntelligence uses the marketing and distribution power of IBM as a means of gaining greater exposure for its products, which consist of two packaged expert systems: (a) Underwriting Advisor, which assists property and casualty insurance underwriters, and (b) Lending Advisor, which helps commercial banks analyze the advisability of making corporate loans. IBM has used this cooperative arrangement as a means of expanding its domain into areas that are not traditionally associated with its data processing orientation.

Guidelines for Senior IS Executives Pursuing Cooperative Arrangements

This chapter argues that cooperative relationships will be increasingly important in positioning IS organizations to contribute effectively to a firm's competitive position. Cooperative arrangements are for those IS organizations that see the need to diversify, to acquire new skills and resources, and to reach objectives that they cannot reach alone.

Many IS organizations reject cooperative arrangements as a way to strengthen their organizations because such arrangements convey that strengthening is needed. An unwillingness to admit that the nature of IS work is changing creates barriers to effective use of cooperative strategies. There are, of course, many other reasons not to consider cooperative arrangements (chief among these are the loss of autonomy and control and the lowering of the internal skill base). However, careful consideration of the production, transaction, and organizational learning costs associated with different cooperative arrangements will help organizations decide whether these reasons are powerful enough to preclude cooperative arrangements. The following is a set

ESTABLISHING COOPERATIVE EXTERNAL RELATIONSHIPS

of guidelines for managers who wish to actively consider cooperative arrangements as a major strategy:

1. Increase your reading to include books on entrepreneurship, intrapreneurship, and joint ventures.
2. Adhere to some basic principles for engaging in cooperative arrangements:
   a. Assess the risk of atrophy of in-house capabilities caused by relying on outside partners to perform some tasks.
   b. Understand that cooperative arrangements involving joint ownership will be most effective if some chemistry between parties can be sparked.
   c. Make sure that the objectives of cooperative arrangement are clear.
   d. Consider production, coordination, and organizational learning costs before deciding on the type of cooperative arrangement.
3. Look for analogies such as the arrangements adopted by some law firms and the advertising staffs of large corporations.
4. Keep informed of what other IS organizations are doing. Rethinking the structure of the IS organization in terms of cooperative arrangements is a radical idea, but as joint arrangements become more prevalent, they will create opportunities to learn from others.
5. Decompose your IS functions into a set of independent activities in order to facilitate acquisition and divestment through market methods. Look for opportunities to divest yourself of activities that have in effect become commodities. Look for opportunities to acquire new knowledge and skills to supplement your own internal strengths.
6. Consider the wide range of available cooperative arrangement options.
7. Make sure the right incentives are in place for divestment. Knowing what to keep, what to give up, and what to acquire is the desired behavior.
8. Be prepared to spend your time differently, since much of your time will be spent in coordination activities associated with these cooperative arrangements.

TRANSFORMING THE IS ORGANIZATION

Notes

1. Williamson, O.E. *Markets and Hierarchies*, New York: Free Press, 1975.
2. Dearden, John. "The Withering Away of the IS Department," *Sloan Management Review*, Summer 1987, pp. 87-91.
3. Allen, Brandt. "Make Information Services Pay Its Way," *Harvard Business Review*, Jan.-Feb. 1987, pp. 57-63.
4. Buday, R. "MIT Professor: MIS Future Lies in Technology, Not Strategy," *Information Week*, June 23, 1986, p. 32.
5. Harrigan, K. *Managing for Joint Venture Success*, Lexington, Mass.: Lexington Books, 1986.
6. Ludlum, David. "Irish Woo Software Operations," *Computerworld*, March 2, 1987, pp. 57-65.
7. Stamps, David. "Is Anyone Really Using Computer Consultants?," *Datamation*, October 15, 1986, pp. 99-102.
8. Chester, Jeffrey A. "A Marriage of Convenience," *Infosystems*, September 1986, pp. 70-72.
9. Hampton, William. "How IBM Wooed Ford Into a More Meaningful Relationship," *Business Week*, March 30, 1987, p. 87.

■
CHAPTER FIVE

MANAGING IS RISK THROUGH OVERSIGHT
MICHAEL J. GINZBERG

Triangle Underwriters Inc., a large insurance broker, signed a contract with Honeywell in April 1970 for a new hardware and software system. The system was installed the end of that year, and from then on almost nothing went right. The system cancelled paid-up policies, recorded unpaid accounts as paid, sent out commissions twice. Within five years, this $1.7 million-a-year business was $250,000 in the red and out of business. (New York Daily News, *August 30, 1980.)*

James A. Cummings Inc., a Fort Lauderdale contractor, sued Lotus Development Corporation in July 1986, charging that an error in Lotus' Symphony software package failed to add $254,000 of G&A costs, causing the company to underbid a $3 million office complex. Lotus reported that the problem was the result of a user error, not a deficiency in the Lotus software; the suit was dropped. (Wall Street Journal, *December 10, 1986.)*

A Texas bus driver being treated for skin cancer died when a software error caused his computer-controlled radiation therapy machine to deliver a dose of radiation 80 times stronger than prescribed. (Wall Street Journal, *January 28, 1987.)*

On May 4, 1982, the British frigate Sheffield was sunk and 20 sailors killed by an Exocet missile fired from an Argentinean aircraft. The Sheffield was equipped with a computerized air defense system designed to detect the radar signals from Soviet bloc missiles. The French-made Exocet, considered "friendly," emits radar signals on the same frequency as the Sheffield's communication system. But because the Sheffield was sending a message to

TRANSFORMING THE IS ORGANIZATION

London at the time, it could not pick up the Exocet's signal. (Wall Street Journal, *January 28, 1987.*)

A computer error blocked the Bank of New York from delivering government securities to customers in late 1985. As a result, the bank had to borrow funds overnight at an interest cost of $5 million. (Wall Street Journal, *January 28, 1987.*)

The new computer system at the New Jersey Division of Motor Vehicles was supposed to improve service to the state's motorists and save $3 million a year in operating costs. Instead, when the system went on-line in 1985, backlogs began to swell while overtime costs increased $160,000 a month. The problem was traced to the programming language used by the outside contractor who built the system. The contractor had chosen to use a fourth generation language for the entire project, even though both the state and the language developer advised against it. The language developer contended that the fourth-generation language could not accommodate the heavy file processing and records transfer sections (about 15 percent) of the system. After several months of using the system, it became apparent the system was hopelessly slow, and the contractor agreed to rewrite some parts in COBOL. (The New York Times, *October 3, 1985.)*

Information technology is increasingly pervasive inside and outside of organizations and its impacts are being felt more widely and more deeply. Malfunctions in information and communication systems can cost an organization large sums of money. For example, one study shows that the loss of their information systems would put most companies out of business in a matter of days. Too many injuries and deaths are already being attributed to the failure of computer-based systems.

The exciting developments in the use of information technology have their price. For instance, they expose companies to new risks. The failure of some piece of the organization's information technology investment could have serious negative consequences for the organization.

Most organizations do not know where the real risks lie in their information services activity. For example, if the courts consider the computer programs that control the runaway radiation therapy machine described earlier to be part of a product rather than a service, the organization that produced it will face a strict standard of absolute liability, not the more lenient standard based on negligence. It is absolutely critical that we recognize the risks *in advance*, and take appropriate protective steps.

What are the critical risks in an organization's information services activity? What must be done to reduce the risk of a failure and mitigate its consequences? Who is responsible for assuring that information systems function correctly (or as correctly as possible)?

Ultimately, a chief information officer must be responsible for *all* information services activity in an organization, even though he cannot directly observe or manage all this activity. This officer will have even less direct control of information services activity in the future, so now is the time to define and adopt appropriate monitoring mechanisms to ensure that the organization's information services activities are properly executed.

Oversight: The Responsibility

What is oversight and why is it necessary? How does it differ (if at all) from internal control as an auditor would define it? What should oversight of the organization's information services activity look like?

In a study of internal controls in more than 600 U.S. organizations,[1] internal control is defined as dealing "with the processes and practices by which the management of an organization attempts to assure that approved and appropriate decisions and activities are made and carried out." Internal control does not necessarily involve direct observation or supervision of an activity or decision-making process. Instead, it is watchful and responsible care for an activity. Internal control, then, provides the feedback necessary to close the loop between planning and action. It involves the exercising of mechanisms to assure that the organization follows the intended path.

Oversight—as defined here—relates to internal control, yet is one level further removed from the organization's activities. Oversight is the meta-control system, the system that assures the existence of effective controls. Consequently, oversight differs in emphasis from internal control; internal control tends to be reactive, oversight is proactive. An organization's oversight system does not just report about events after the fact, it provides timely monitoring and alerting for possible redirection (or cessation) of ongoing activities. In short, oversight (a) assures that critical risks are identified, and (b) provides a system for monitoring risky activities so as to alert management to dangers before they become problems. The oversight system must

101

also provide a set of measures for activities that are measurable, inspection procedures for those that are not measurable, and a way to differentiate between the two.

Why Is Oversight Necessary?

Large, complicated organizations need oversight to assure that the actions of many individuals are effectively coordinated and properly directed toward the achievement of the organization's ends. The larger, more complex, and more dynamic an organization, the greater the need for a carefully conceived oversight system. Oversight also helps ensure that the actions of individuals do not expose the organization to risks it does not wish to assume. In sum, the oversight process guards against unacceptable increases in organizational entropy.

Oversight of an organization's information services activities is especially critical because in addition to being large and complex, IS is widespread and expensive. The people involved work in many parts of an organization, not only in a central IS department but in divisional IS departments and other functional (user) departments as well. In many organizations, IS expenditures constitute a significant—and the fastest growing—portion of the budget. As a major user of an organization's capital, information services requires substantial long-term investments in facilities that often must be made long before the demand for those facilities appear.

As pointed out in the opening chapter, upper management has often had bad experiences and unpleasant surprises with information services in the past. Indeed, some non-IS managers have poor intuition when it comes to information services. They fail to realize that $1 spent on development implies $3 to be spent on maintenance and countless other dollars for operations. They still do not understand that a "90 percent complete" system may still require more time and money to finish—if it's ever finished—than has been spent already. In situations like these, an oversight system for monitoring progress and adherence to plans ensures moving things in the intended direction at the intended pace.

Finally, information services is now consequential. Doing it right really matters. Ten years ago a data processing failure might have meant a missed payroll. While such failures were clearly embarrassing and annoying (and perhaps a legal headache!), companies and individuals would survive. However, ten years from now an IS failure will likely have the same impact as an earthquake measuring 8.5 on the

MANAGING IS RISK THROUGH OVERSIGHT

Richter scale and centered on your most critical production facility; the organization may not be able to recover.

Unfortunately, there is no tradition of oversight in the information services area. Instead there is after-the-fact reporting. Independent projects or operations are launched and are expected to produce results with little if any monitoring of the activities that lead to those results. This holds true within an IS department (consider the abysmal project management systems in use in many organizations), and even more so in the relationship of the IS department to the rest of the organization.

General management has not been involved with IS. The information services activity has largely been left to monitor itself, except for the occasional intrusion of internal auditors. Other organizations have used a market mechanism instead of explicit oversight. By treating IS units as profit centers, success in a competitive environment can take the place of explicitly monitoring a unit's activities. IS units are seldom dealt with in this manner, which is also not an adequate way to monitor and control information services activities. Looking at the results of competition is entirely after-the-fact and retrospective. It reports successes or failures, although seldom in time to alter course. The potential cost of an information services failure is just too great for a company to wait for after-the-fact confirmation from the marketplace. Early warning mechanisms are needed to identify failures before they occur and to turn them around.

A system for oversight of *all* the information services activities in an organization can provide senior management with a level of comfort concerning this vital piece of the organization. Regardless of whether a company treats IS activities as decentralized profit centers or highly centralized, an ongoing oversight program—monitoring, alerting, assuring—is necessary. Oversight must ensure that the organization's information services activity—not just the IS department—is doing the right work and getting it done right.

Who Is Responsible for Oversight of IS?

By now it should be apparent that oversight of an organization's information services activities is essential, but who is responsible for this process? Is there—should there be—one person who is responsible?

Few organizations today have a single individual with direct line authority over all these activities. In many organizations, authority for

TRANSFORMING THE IS ORGANIZATION

all information services activities occurs only at the CEO level. Indeed, senior management must take responsibility for oversight of information services. The IS activity has (or will) become too important to most organizations for senior management not to take this responsibility. The CEO, however, has many other concerns and frequently lacks the knowledge and experience necessary to personally direct, guide, or watch over the information services activity.

The CEO, then, can choose for oversight of the separate clusters of information services to occur at the local level only, or delegate that responsibility to some other member of the senior management team. But this really is no choice. The first approach, complete "local" autonomy, is not adequate today, and it will be even less so ten years from now. Thus, central oversight must be provided by a senior manager knowledgeable enough about both the business and about the technology, usually a chief information officer.

Oversight of information services is technology dependent. The nature of the oversight process will change as the activity being monitored changes. Thus, the executive responsible for the process must understand the underlying technological activity.

Such delegation of responsibility fits with the recommendations of recent studies of internal control. The Canadian Institute of Chartered Accountants, for example, has concluded that "control of information systems is the responsibility of senior management".[2] But since executing this responsibility qualifies as a distributed activity, senior management should play the design role of planning, policy setting, and assigning responsibilities to ensure an effective system for IS planning and control. Execution responsibility, however, rests with the users of information services activities. Exhibit 5-1 presents another way to view this division of responsibilities. Top management, represented by the CIO, has oversight responsibility, i.e., responsibility for assuring the existence of effective controls, for all IS activity throughout the organization. Responsibility for executing controls is distributed. For activities involving the technology platform, the responsibility rests with the IS manager directly in charge of that activity (in some cases, this may be the CIO); for activities involving the business platform, the responsibility belongs to the business manager in charge of that area of the business.

In summary, central oversight of all information services activity in an organization is critical, and it can best be provided by a chief information officer. The CIO cannot be directly in control of all IS activity (and in fact may not have line control of any of this activity);

Exhibit 5-1. Oversight and Control Responsibility for IS Activity

	Executing Controls	Assuring Existence of Effective Controls
Technology Platform	IS Manager	CIO
Business Platform	Business Manager	CIO

hence, he must define a set of procedures and mechanisms to provide adequate oversight without requiring direct control. These procedures and mechanisms should be carried out jointly by personnel throughout the organization, including the CIO, other IS personnel, the users of information services, and internal auditors.

Oversight in IS Today

Research indicates that the extent of formalized IS oversight today is limited. Oversight of central information services activity is the most developed, especially in large organizations. These central IS organizations are staffed by information services professionals who are aware of the need for

1. Physical control of the data processing facility;
2. Appropriate assignment of responsibilities (for example, separating programming and operating roles);
3. Development methodologies that ensure adequate testing and maintainability; and
4. Program change controls.

These procedures and mechanisms satisfy an auditor's need for control, but the profile of existing controls indicates the absence of any comprehensive system of oversight even for the central IS activity.

The Mautz et al. study of internal control in major U.S. corporations

Exhibit 5-2. Control Exposure of Systems as Ranked by IS Managers

Rank	System
1	Accounts payable
2	Payroll
3	Accounts receivable
4	Inventory
5	Sales, order entry, credit and billing
6	Shareholder records
7	Engineering and scientific data
8	Financial management and forecasting
9	Loan processing and insurance claims
10	Personnel
11	Litigation support

Source: Table 3 from *Internal Control in U.S. Corporations*, by R.K. Mantz, W.G. Kell, M.W. Maher, A.G. Merten, R.R. Reilly, D.G. Severance, and B.J. White. Adapted by permission of Financial Executives Research Foundation.

identified which systems IS managers believed presented the greatest "exposure," (the most significant risk to the organization) and thus were systems where control should be focused. The results of the study, reproduced in Exhibit 5-2, indicate that IS managers focus largely on the typical transaction processing systems, especially those that deal directly with cash or physical assets. Other operational systems and systems that support decision-making ranked much lower—as presenting much less exposure—if they ranked at all. As the examples at the beginning of this chapter suggest, these non-accounting systems may in fact present an organization with risk at least as great as that of the traditional accounting and transaction processing systems.

The above, of course, deals with the *central* information services activity. When looking at distributed information services activities—whether departmental computers, personal computers, or end-user development—the situation worsens considerably. While many organizations have adopted standards for distributed information services activity—for example, hardware or software standards, a common development methodology, and security and back-up procedures—enforcement of those standards is at best problematic.

MANAGING IS RISK THROUGH OVERSIGHT

A CIO can issue standards and set procedures, yet in most cases he cannot enforce them (a symptom of the "whipping post" problem discussed in Chapter 3). Add to this that the people doing information processing throughout the organization do not understand the need for these procedures; they see them as an additional expense that provides no additional benefit. Their lack of information processing experience leads them to underestimate the potential for trouble, which only multiplies the problems. Not only does inexperience lead these people to ignore the procedures that could save them when a problem arises, but it increases the probability that they will make a mistake that creates a problem.

Designing an Oversight System for Information Services

The first step to designing an effective oversight system is agreeing that oversight of the organization's information services activities is necessary. The next step: consider the details of the system's design. Before considering the specific areas for, or mechanisms of, oversight, managers must first understand some basic principles for design.

Principles of Oversight for Information Services

Seven interrelated principles guide the design of an oversight system for an organization's information services activities:

1. The IS oversight system should be proactive and anticipatory.
2. The IS oversight system should be flexible and adaptive.
3. The IS oversight system should be custom designed.
4. The IS oversight system should be oriented toward critical risks.
5. The IS oversight system should be a minimal system.
6. The IS oversight system should inform and influence behavior of information services and user personnel.
7. Execution of IS oversight should be a shared task among management, IS, and user personnel.

Proactive and anticipatory. To date, the control systems for information processing activity have been almost exclusively after-the-fact reporting systems. Chargeback systems, post-project reviews, and profit center structures have all enabled us to keep score of what happened

TRANSFORMING THE IS ORGANIZATION

in the past, but provide little guidance for the present. They offer a mechanism for assigning blame when things go wrong, but not for directing them to success.

The IS oversight system must be an anticipatory system. Rather than evaluating and reporting what happened, it must monitor where the activity is going. Instead of assigning blame when problems arise, it must trigger corrective action to force success. In short, it must focus on managing toward desired outcomes. This in turn requires designing the IS oversight system as part of the IS planning process; in essence, oversight is built into each activity at the planning stage.

Flexible and adaptive. The oversight mechanism must match the nature of the activity being monitored; that is, the oversight for a system under development is different from that for a running application system. Similarly, a payroll system likely exhibits different oversight demands than does a decision support system used in R&D labs. The oversight mechanisms employed need to be as varied, flexible, and dynamic as the information services activities themselves.

Custom designed. No two organizations have exactly the same set of information services activities, nor do they operate in the same environment. To be effective, oversight mechanisms must fit the activity being monitored, the technology being used, and the environment in which the activity is occurring. Thus, the IS oversight system should be unique to each organization at a specific point in time, custom designed for that setting.

Oriented toward critical risks. The fundamental purpose of an IS oversight system is risk management, but what real risks does an organization face? The traditional approach to assessing the need for control of information services activities is borrowed from auditors. It focuses first on financial statements and the systems that produce them. At one time, control was considered to be adequate if it assured that the "numbers" in those systems were correct. More recently, particularly following passage of the Foreign Corrupt Practices Act, protection of assets has become an additonal criterion for determining the need for control. While these financial orientations no doubt identify some important areas for oversight, the potential for disaster arising from nonfinancial systems can be equally critical. Consider the following (in some cases hypothetical, but in all cases plausible) examples of nonfinancial systems and the impacts their failures could have:

Operational Systems

- Automated train dispatching system used by Southern Railway (*Interfaces*, December 1983)
- Union Carbide Bhopal plant maintenance scheduling system (hypothetical)

Decision Support Systems

- Simulation model used by Morton Thiokol for the O-ring analysis used in the Challenger space shuttle design (hypothetical)
- Acquisition evaluation model used by a large aerospace firm

Expert Systems

- Intelligent plant scheduling system used by a major electronics firm
- Medical diagnosis systems (e.g., MYCIN, INTERNIST-1, McDope) used as consultants by physicians (*Wall Street Journal*, July 8, 1987)

Traditional auditing practice would not focus on these nonfinancial systems, but each presents a risk potentially more damaging to an organization than many financial systems.

The evolution of computer use in organizations has changed the risk situation. In addition to the concerns about certain application systems, key risks now exist in such areas as personnel—does the organization have appropriate personnel and IS skills available to meet its current and future needs; timing—will critical application systems and platform technologies be in place and available when the need for them arises; and resource acquisition and utilization—are valuable information resources including personnel and data being acquired and are they being properly deployed and managed.

The IS oversight system must deal with all these risk areas. It must not only recognize the existence of a given risk, but also the magnitude of that risk, so that appropriate action can be taken. Management must focus its attention on large risks, especially in areas where failures would require a long time to fix or from which it would be difficult to recover. Further, since oversight has a cost and is not available in infinite supply, an organization must be selective and direct its oversight efforts to the most critical areas. As indicated above, the critical areas now are not always the ones focused upon in the past.

TRANSFORMING THE IS ORGANIZATION

Minimal system. Oversight is not costless and does not of itself produce any added value to the organization. Because of risks, however, organizations cannot get by without it. The key, then, is to make the oversight—and the control—system as small and unobtrusive as possible; to adopt the minimal oversight system compatible with the risks the organization faces and with the risk level management is willing to assume.

We can follow several guidelines to produce an acceptable minimal oversight system. The first was suggested above: design the system to focus on the key risks. Rather than monitoring and reporting on every information services activity in the organization, today's organizations must confine active monitoring and reporting to the subset of activities that present the greatest risks.

Next, they must recognize that many oversight mechanisms are available, each differing in their cost as well as their capabilities. Plans, standards, and guidelines are at the base of the oversight system and are perhaps the least expensive of all oversight mechanisms. Routine reports using standard measures are relatively inexpensive oversight mechanisms, and are appropriate if the activity being monitored is basically standard and stable. Nonstandard activities and activities undergoing substantial change require more direct inspection for effective oversight. Inspection, of course, is more costly than standard reporting. The key lies in matching the oversight mechanism to the activity, with the goal of minimizing the size and cost of the monitoring system while maintaining adequate oversight. In general, there is no reason to spend more on oversight than the benefit it provides by lowering risk.

Inform and influence behavior. The oversight system is effective only if it leads people to act consistently with the organization's interests. Any measurement system impacts behavior by *what* it measures (observes, reports on) and *how* it measures those objects. Thus, the oversight system provides significant incentives. Does it encourage people to play the new roles deemed necessary, or does it work against them? Does it align authority and responsibility for information services activities in a manner consistent with the organization's IS mission? Does the system support the necessary partnerships within the organization, or does it make them disadvantageous to one of the partners? Does it support joint venturing, acquisition, and divestment of IS activities, or does it favor the status quo? The key here is that the

MANAGING IS RISK THROUGH OVERSIGHT

IS oversight system must be consistent with and supportive of the organization's plan and direction.

Shared execution. IS oversight, even when well designed and kept to a minimum, will be too large an activity for any one person or group. *Responsibility* for IS oversight should rest with the CIO for two reasons: (1) The CIO is the chief technologist and the system must be driven by the technology in use, and (2) the CIO is in the best position to have a broad, encompassing perspective of the organization's information services activity. Operation of the system, however, must be shared by IS and user personnel.

For example, one aspect of the IS oversight system might be to assure that adequate telecommunications network capacity is always available to the organization. While IS can reasonably be expected to convert user activity plans to network volumes and to provide capacity accordingly, IS cannot be expected to know that users are about to change their activities in a way that affects volumes. Keeping IS apprised of plans as they relate to information services activities is one part of users' responsibilities for making an oversight system work.

IS Activities Subject to Oversight

The aforementioned seven principles provide broad guidance for designing a system that ensures the organization's information services activity functions properly. However, we have not yet addressed just *what* activities those are. For defining oversight needs it helps to look at information services activity along two orthogonal dimensions: work content and work flow.

A Work Content View of Oversight

The first dimension along which we can look at information services activities is work content, or the specific processes involved in IS activities. Three related sets of IS processes need to be considered: development, operations, and building the technology platform.

Development focuses on the application system design and implementation processes. The oversight issues for these processes include:

- Are the right systems being developed?
- Is sharing and reuse of systems and modules being accomplished and duplication avoided?

TRANSFORMING THE IS ORGANIZATION

- Are systems being developed in a way that assures their correctness and maintainability?
- Are the systems being developed returning sufficient benefits to justify the investment in them?

Operations focuses on the day-to-day processes of making application systems available to users and keeping those systems up to date. This includes "delivery" of the application on an appropriate computer system, the actual running of that computer system, and the ongoing maintenance of the application program. Oversight questions in this area include:

- Are application systems being delivered through an appropriate vehicle (computer system) and will they continue to be?
- What is being done to assure that application system maintenance occurs and is properly controlled?
- Are application systems being used correctly, both for their intended purpose and according to plan?
- Are steps being taken to assure the quality and integrity of the organization's data resources?
- Are hardware systems being managed to assure continued proper functioning?

Building the technology platform focuses on the long-term and broad processes of assuring that the organization maintains adequate hardware, software, and communications technology bases to enable it to meet both existing and emerging needs for information services. The types of oversight issues this raises include:

- Are the hardware and software architectures, the communications network, and the organization's databases capable of meeting current and foreseeable future needs?
- Will the architectures, networks, and databases be adequate to meet as yet unforeseen needs?
- Is there adequate security of the technology platform (architectures, networks, and databases)?

A Workflow View of Oversight

Each of the preceding IS processes goes through a series of stages. The stages are not necessarily linear; iteration can occur among the stages, but, ultimately, each process must pass through each stage.

MANAGING IS RISK THROUGH OVERSIGHT

The second dimension of information services activity, the workflow dimension, focuses on these process stages.

The first process stage is planning, determining what needs to be done: what technologies to employ, what applications to develop, when to put technologies and applications in place. The relationship between planning and oversight is complex. We stated earlier that the planning process must include planning for appropriate oversight mechanisms for all key information services activities. Now we need to recognize the other side of the planning-oversight relationship. *The oversight system must ensure that the planning system and planning process are in place and functioning.* Making sure that the planning process works addresses the issue of timing risk identified earlier.

Once work has been planned, someone must be responsible for carrying it out. In a traditional, centralized data processing organization, assigning responsibilities is relatively easy. In the merging IS environment, assuring that every activity has someone responsible for it is not so simple. An earlier chapter describes the set of relationships, both within the firm and external to it, that characterize the IS activity. Responsibility for IS activity is distributed across that network of relationships so the oversight system must assure that someone somewhere in the network has responsibility for everything that must be done. Being explicit about these responsibility assignments begins to address the personnel risk discussed in the previous section.

Once responsibility is assigned, the necessary resources must be available. The oversight system must assure that resources are acquired and made available when and where they are needed and at a reasonable cost. Attending to this stage addresses resource acquisition risk.

Finally, the work must get done. The network of relationships, both within the firm and external to it, is again of particular relevance. Much of the work to be accomplished occurs at a relationship boundary and involves people from two or more groups. The oversight system, then, must assure that relationships are working and are properly structured to encourage and facilitate the actions necessary to get the work done. Assuring proper task execution addresses the issue of resource utilization risk.

To summarize in terms of workflow, the oversight system for information services must see that

1. The planning is done and is properly informed about risks and trade-offs;

TRANSFORMING THE IS ORGANIZATION

2. Responsibility is assigned and accepted;
3. Where trust is placed, it is justified (that is, there is reason to believe that the work *can* be accomplished); and
4. The work is under control both economically and in the sense of contingency planning.

Information Services Activities Matrix

The IS workflow and work content dimensions can be juxtaposed to create a two-dimensional view of information services activities. This matrix provides a useful way to look at IS when considering oversight needs. Each call in the matrix presents an identifiable and essentially different activity which potentially presents a unique set of oversight needs. Exhibit 5-3 presents the matrix and identifies some representative oversight issues. Oversight needs differ among development, operations, and platform building activities; and, they differ across the stages for any one of the activities. Design of the oversight system, then, must take into account the specific activity involved.

To complete the picture, remember that oversight of the information services activity is required no matter where in the organization that activity occurs or which technology it involves. Thus, each cell of the matrix may be repeated in several contexts—central, departmental, individual—and for many systems. The need for oversight remains essentially the same regardless of whether it is the general ledger system being developed and run on the corporation's mainframe computer by the central, professional information services department, or a stress analysis model written in BASIC and run on a PC by an engineer in the product development laboratories. However, the appropriate oversight mechanisms may well differ.

Mechanisms for Oversight

The piece still missing from our oversight puzzle is an understanding of the mechanisms that can be employed to provide the needed oversight, and where each mechanism fits. Fundamental to this understanding is the recognition that people are the heart of the oversight system; oversight can be accomplished effectively only through people. Thus, questions of motivation, goal perception, and the appropriateness of rewards are at least as important as the technical characteristics

Exhibit 5-3. Information Services Activities Matrix: Representative Oversight Issues

	Development	Operations	Platform Building
Planning	• Application risk assessment • Portfolio planning	• Capacity forecasting • Delivery guidelines	• Demand forecasting • Architecture planning
Responsibility assignment	• Project leadership • Inter-project communication	• Maintenance assignments • Change control	• User liaison roles • New technology introduction
Resource availability	• Developer training • Skills Inventory • Development environment	• Capacity management • Skills inventory • Physical security • Data integrity	• Technology assessment and forecasting • New technology acquisition
Task execution	• Project progress tracking • Compliance to standards • Project impact	• Operations monitoring and review • Maintenance review	• Technological "readiness"

of the mechanisms. For example, a technically superior mechanism that is viewed by those who use it as not in their best interests is likely to be ineffective. On the other hand, simple mechanisms can be effective if they are viewed favorably and embraced by the people who must make them work.

The mechanisms of oversight are essentially the mechanisms used to provide control (recall that oversight is the process of assuring that an adequate and effective control system is in place); thus, the manifestation of oversight *is* the planning and control system. Because of the need to tailor an oversight system to the characteristics of the specific setting in which it will be operating, we cannot specify a precise mapping of oversight tools to information services activities. We can, however, develop an understanding of the types of mechanisms that are available and what can be accomplished with those mechanisms.

Oversight mechanisms can be divided into five major groups:

TRANSFORMING THE IS ORGANIZATION

1. *Protective measures,* including standards (e.g., for hardware, software, development, documentation), expenditure limits, and security systems (e.g., physical security, access control);
2. *Organization,* including reporting relationships, responsibility assignments (e.g., for files, application systems), job descriptions, and separation of functions;
3. *Training* of personnel both within and outside of the IS function;
4. *Reports and records,* including routine status reports, project progress reports, and change reports; and
5. *Reviews and inspections,* including audits, walkthroughs, and other first-hand reviews of people and systems.

These five classes of oversight mechanisms differ in

- How expensive they are to apply;
- Preventive vs. detective orientation;
- Time frame of feedback provided;
- Sensitivity and adaptability to change;
- Dependence on the skill or knowledge of the user.

The first of these dimensions is self-explanatory, while the others require some explanation. A *preventive* oversight mechanism attempts to set up the conditions that can keep problems from arising, but it does not necessarily provide any help for finding or correcting any problems that do arise. Essentially, these are passive mechanisms. A more active *detective* mechanism aims at identifying problems as they arise.

Time frame of feedback refers to the timeliness of the information provided by the oversight mechanism; that is, if the mechanism provides any feedback information at all, how close in time to the events it represents is that information?

Sensitivity and adaptability to change concerns the degree to which the mechanism is static or dynamic. Some oversight mechanisms are "tuned" to the conditions existing when they are first put in place, and neither recognize nor respond to changes in their surrounding conditions. Other mechanisms are sensitive to changes in their environments and can alter their functioning to accommodate these environmental changes.

For some oversight mechanisms, the only impact of the person applying the mechanism is in deciding whether or not to use the mechanism. These mechanisms, once activated, essentially operate independently of the specific human operator (rules, standards, and

MANAGING IS RISK THROUGH OVERSIGHT

routine reports are examples). For other mechanisms, the *skill and knowledge of the operator* influence the mechanism's effectiveness. The operation of these latter mechanisms is non-routine and requires skilled human intervention.

Exhibit 5-4 depicts the characteristics of the five classes of oversight mechanism along these five dimensions.

If we think of oversight mechanisms as organized in some sort of hierarchy, *protective measures* and *organization* (structuring) fall to the bottom end. They are inexpensive, preventive mechanisms that once in place do not rely on skilled users to function. Basic to an organization's IS oversight system, they outline the requirement for and structurally enable planning, assignment of responsibility, and acquisition of resources across all three major processes; development, operations, and platform building. These mechanisms are essential to all of the oversight issues raised earlier, because they establish the "laws" that govern action; for example, they establish policies and procedures for software sharing, system delivery vehicle selection, technology platform planning and evolution. Protective measures and organization provide the base for the oversight system; but they cannot provide complete oversight in any situation, because they are essentially passive mechanisms providing no feedback and totally insensitive to change.

Training comprises the next level of the hierarchy. While *organization*

Exhibit 5-4. Characteristics of Oversight Mechanisms

Major Groups of Mechanisms	Expense of Application	Preventive/ Detective	Time Frame of Feedback	Sensitivity to Change	Dependence on Skill and Knowledge
Protective Measures	Low	Preventive	None	Very low	Low
Organization	Low	Preventive	None	Very low	Low
Training	Medium	Preventive	Long	Low	Medium
Reports and Records	Low to medium	Detective	Variable (often long)	Low	Low
Reviews and Inspections	High	Detective	Variable (can be very short)	High	High

117

TRANSFORMING THE IS ORGANIZATION

structurally enables oversight, that oversight mission cannot be executed unless people are adequately prepared to do so. Training is needed for the people involved in each of the activities and at each stage in the IS activities matrix: users, managers, and IS personnel who must plan and carry out development, operations, and platform building activities. This mix calls for a wide range of types of training, including training in the use of specific programming tools, development methodologies, and planning systems.

Like the preceding mechanisms, training has a preventive orientation and is relatively insensitive to environmental change—at least in the short run. The nature of training makes it somewhat dependent on a trainer's skill and knowledge; i.e. delivery, though not necessarily content, depends on the trainer. And, because there is a person actively involved in the delivery mechanism, there is some opportunity for feedback from the environment, though not necessarily rapid feedback. Training is a key oversight mechanism because unless people are trained to properly carry out their tasks, it is foolish to expect that they will. In other words, wishing and hoping are not adequate substitutes for direct, positive action.

If the world were benign, if people always did exactly and only what they were told to, if organizational environments were tranquil, then protective measures, organization, and training would be all that was needed to provide IS oversight. However, the world is not that way so other oversight mechanisms are needed.

Reports and records form the next step in the hierarchy. These mechanisms differ in a very fundamental way from the three already discussed. They have a detective, rather than preventive, orientation; they are used to monitor the success of the other mechanisms. Among the detective mechanisms, the strengths of reports and records are relatively low cost and low dependence on user skill; that is, user skill is not critical because these mechanisms rely on standard measures and routine data collection procedures. But reliance on standard measures and routine procedures is also the mechanisms' weakness. Routine reports are not sensitive to change in their environment, and the feedback they provide is often not rapid. Such reports may be adequate to monitor progress on a well-defined system development project, but they are not likely to suffice for assuring the adequacy of the technology platform planning process.

At the top level of the oversight mechanism hierarchy lie *reviews and inspections*. Like reports and records, these are detective mechanisms; but, unlike the previous mechanisms, reviews and inspections

MANAGING IS RISK THROUGH OVERSIGHT

are quite sensitive to environmental change and can provide very rapid feedback. The negatives, of course, are expense of application and high dependence on user (the inspector) skill. These are the mechanisms which must be used to monitor the more uncertain, novel information services activities, e.g., the development of an expert system using a new methodology.

To summarize, these five groups of oversight mechanisms form a hierarchy. As we move up the hierarchy, from protective measures to reviews and inspections:

- The cost of the mechanisms generally increases;
- The organizational scope of the mechanisms—the range of problems they can address—increases;
- The information processing capacity of the mechanisms increases; and
- The ability of the mechanisms to deal with uncertainty and to handle exceptions increases.

As indicated earlier, the selection of specific oversight mechanisms must be determined by the situation for which oversight is required. That is, the detailed standards, job descriptions, content of training and reports, etc., must be situation specific. The hierarchy of mechanisms outlined above, however, can provide guidance for selecting the types of mechanisms to employ.

One final point should be made about the design of the oversight system. All that has been discussed so far assumes that reasonable people will be able to reach agreement about objectives and the means to achieve them; that the person who must make the oversight mechanism work and the person who has ultimate oversight responsibility share a view of the importance of and need for oversight. In a distributed information services environment, this is unlikely; at times, there will be irreconcilable differences. The end user who is asked to attend two weeks of training before developing a LOTUS spreadsheet might prefer just getting down to work and experimenting with the tool; he does not understand how easy it is to make serious, difficult-to-detect errors with such powerful tools. The manager of a departmental development group may not want to incur the extra cost of using the central IS department's life cycle development methodology; after all, it is the manager who is responsible for the budget.

The CIO cannot just abandon these situations and often does not have the authority to force a resolution to his liking. So, what can or should be done? The answer is to put "teeth" into the oversight process, to make oversight a firm requirement rather than something to be done only if time or extra budget allows. Top management must make the mandate for oversight clear and must indicate its willingness to serve as a "court of last resort" to resolve any disputes about oversight. The experience reported by organizations who have taken such an approach suggests that it works—not because the CEO spends time mediating disputes, but because everyone realizes that oversight should be taken seriously.

Summary and Agenda for Action

The purpose of this chapter has been to establish the need for a system of oversight for an organization's information services activities. We have identified why oversight is necessary, shown that existing control mechanisms for information services generally fall short of what is needed, and provided guidelines and a framework for developing an IS oversight system.

That oversight system must be concerned with more than just the content and correctness of application systems. It must also address the timing, personnel, and resource risks in order to assure readiness and faultless operation of the technology platform. Thus, it is substantially broader than the quality assurance programs for IS that a number of organizations have adopted. In addition to addressing what *is* being done, oversight must consider what *is not* being done.

To reiterate, developing an IS oversight system is not a matter of establishing a formal chain of command and assigning responsibility so that someone may be held accountable after the fact. The issue is identifying and managing the organization's information-services-related risks while they still are risks, not problems. The purpose of oversight is anticipation, not retribution. It must be built into the planning process for information services, not added on as an afterthought once plans are in place.

How can an organization move from its current state to such an oversight system? Four major steps are required. The first is to *sell the concept* of oversight. Centrally directed oversight of all information services activities in an organization is an idea that will not be warmly embraced by everyone in an organization. The importance of the idea must be made evident; the risk of not doing it must be made clear. The sale must be made to managers throughout the organization but it must be made first at the very top. If top management does not

MANAGING IS RISK THROUGH OVERSIGHT

accept the idea, does not embrace the need for IS oversight, and is not willing to say so to the rest of the organization, the oversight system will never work.

Once the concept has been sold, the rest of the process is much easier, though perhaps more time consuming. The second step is to *identify critical IS risks*. Where are the risks this organization faces at this time? The nature and magnitude of risks across the full range of information services activities must be assessed. If that assessment is done carefully, the results are likely to show that critical risks to the organization exist in areas that were not previously considered risky.

The third step is to *structure the oversight system around critical risks*. This is likely to be a multi-stage, incremental task. It begins with instituting the first-level enabling mechanisms (protective measures, organization, and training), then adding reporting and monitoring, starting with the areas of the greatest risk. Eventually a complete system should be put in place with the proper balance between risk and cost.

Finally, *the oversight system must be monitored and evolved*. Building the system once is not enough. Continued attention is required to ensure that it is being used properly, and to determine when changes are required. The examples at the beginning of this chapter illustrate dramatic failures of oversight systems. By the time such failures occur, however, it is too late. The oversight system must serve as an *early warning system*. For this to occur, continued assurance is needed that the oversight system itself is working, which requires continuous checking and monitoring. Oversight, once built into the functioning of an organization, must be an ongoing and ever-changing process.

Notes

1. Mautz, R.K., W.G. Kell, M.W. Maher, A.G. Merten, R.R. Reilly, D.G. Severance, and B.J. White. *Internal Control in U.S. Corporations: The State of the Art*, Financial Executives Research Foundation, New York, 1980.
2. Rosen, R.J., G.R. Baker, R.H. Healy, and D.W. Rogers. *Computer Control Guidelines* (2nd edition), Canadian Institute of Chartered Accountants, 1986.

CHAPTER SIX

QUESTIONS AND ANSWERS ABOUT TRANSFORMING AN IS ORGANIZATION

ICIT Research Study Team #1 originally presented its findings in September 1987 as part of a two-day conference in Washington, D.C. After each day's presentations, the conference attendees met in small groups to discuss the presentations and prepare questions for the research team members. This chapter reflects the questions, concerns, and issues raised at the conference and the researchers' post-conference reactions.

1. How can the IS executive become accepted as part of the senior management team?

Both the senior management team and the IS executive can reap great benefits from learning to communicate and forming partnerships. The IS executive needs to attain the political authority and legitimacy necessary to manage IS as a strategic part of the business; senior managers need to be able to understand the implications of IS to their firm and to the markets within which they compete. Mutual understanding is the key to bridging these two roles.

Senior management can learn to appreciate the role of IS in the organization by understanding more fully the value of IS. This objective can be met in two ways: (a) steering committee meetings held for the purpose of briefing the senior management team on IS issues can help increase the level of awareness; and (b) an emphasis on IS-related education for senior management can build mutual understanding and facilitate change through IS. Understanding and education can help senior management to stop viewing IS as merely another expense; it is important that the IS executive drive and promote these activities.

IS executives, as they endeavor to be fully accepted by senior management, must begin to think and act like managers rather than technicians. Language is a place to start: IS managers can learn to relate to senior management team members with business-oriented language rather than with technical jargon. Also, it may be necessary for IS executives to supplement existing technical skills with business and organizational skills through some educational programs. To further promote the partnership with senior management, IS executives should create an IS mission framed in terms of the wider corporate goals as well as the core business drivers. Finally, the IS executive must be able to justify the use and necessity of IS in business terms—the terms senior management best understands.

2. How does a manager of IS avoid the erosion of technical skills in decentralization?

The answer to this question depends on the specific career trajectory of each IS professional, since not all IS-business hybrids will require the same level of technical knowledge and currency. For the more business-oriented hybrid, technical skills will play a distinctly minor role. However, for the technology-oriented hybrid, this issue is of genuine concern. The integration of computing and communications requires an increased depth of technical experience as well as an expansive currency of technical expertise. This, however, is now coupled with an erosion in the *value* of these skills and experiences. The IS world changes so frequently that being an "old timer" in the field is becoming less valuable. The best weapon against skill erosion in any organization structure is education. Chapter 1 cites specific examples of appropriate courses and training. In any case, any IS-focused education program must meet three criteria: skill maintenance, new skill development, and personal growth and innovation.

Technical skills are not the only skills worth protecting or enhancing; maintaining business and functional knowledge is equally important, particularly for understanding nontechnical aspects of the work system (workers, ergonomics, and organizational procedures). Additional skills to be nurtured include communicating and listening well, and acting as both an educator and a consultant.

QUESTIONS AND ANSWERS

3. Is it necessary to educate or hybridize *all* IS professionals and, if so, how does one do it?

The IS organization is filling an increasingly strategic role in firms, but few IS organizations provide the necessary skill set and associated career structure that allow the IS professional to support IS's changing role. In order for a firm to succeed, IS professionals will need to work with business units on a much different basis. Rather than a user/service provider relationship, business units and IS will relate as client/colleague. This relationship will require both hybrid IS professionals and hybrid line managers. The "how" of this question will be accomplished by an increased emphasis on and support for education. In addition, firms will need to reevaluate IS recruiting practices to include candidates with non-technical backgrounds. Finally, incentives and procedures must be established to facilitate and encourage transfers into and out of IS to increase the hybridization process.

4. How can the right incentives be established so that IS will accept the risks and costs of developing effective partnerships with business units?

Several factors are necessary in order to create an environment conducive to forming partnerships. The first factor in developing the IS/business unit relationship is the support and encouragement of senior management, which takes the form of fiscal and political support for projects; a statement of mission clarifying the importance of these relationships; and the reward and promotion of significant efforts. In addition, opportunities for IS and line managers to work across divisional boundaries are necessary. IS and line managers must trust and perceive each other as organizational equals in order to behave as partners, and the organization as a whole must commit to sponsoring the partnership through formal and informal managerial mechanisms such as task forces and advisory boards. However, for the best results, a middle ground must be reached in the organization's use of formal and informal mechanisms. Formal mechanisms can lead to a decrease in a participant's level of dedication to the partnership; informal mechanisms can be responsible for a waning of the partnership's efficiency and usefulness.

The concept of partnering cannot be forced on managers. Instead, the environment, support system, rewards and promotions, and positive reinforcement should foster partnerships by allowing IS and the business units to incur this risk as an informed risk. And as with any other informed risk, there are two potential outcomes: possible failure or probable success.

5. How can technical managers be encouraged to take risks?

Any organization that supports an individual's freedom to fail must give managers the authority to make an informed decision concerning a risky yet innovative venture. In such an organization, a manager will not be punished for an unsuccessful project based on an informed risk. However, there is risk inherent in success just as in failure. Frequently, a successful innovation for one manager may signal a loss of power or resources for another manager through the shifting and reorganizing of resources. The freedom to succeed means that the "losing" manager affected by the change will not risk losing anything personally in terms of compensation, advancement, or status.

In order to elicit this kind of risk-taking behavior, the organization must earn the trust and cooperation of its managers by providing a climate conducive to the freedom to succeed and the freedom to fail. Moreover an organization committed to building this kind of environment will provide its managers with the authority and responsibility to perform their tasks, sufficient resources to complete them, and recognition for their success.

6. How is oversight distinguished from what many companies call quality assurance?

Quality assurance and oversight are related, but oversight is a broader, higher level process. As stated before, oversight is the process of assuring the existence of an appropriate set of controls for IS activities. Surely, one piece of this set is the systems and procedures that guarantee quality service. In other words, one role of the oversight system would be to assure the existence and proper functioning of the quality assurance system. There are several ways to conceptualize the differences between oversight and quality assurance. Oversight should be very proactive, with an emphasis on determining *in advance* where the risks are and assuring that proper precautions are taken. Quality assurance is more reactive, monitoring the outcomes of ongoing ac-

QUESTIONS AND ANSWERS

tivities to assure that they are functioning well. Oversight is concerned not only with what the organization is doing, but with what it is *not* doing; that is, does failing to have certain systems or activities in place present a risk to the organization? Quality assurance should focus only on the existing set of systems and activities. Finally, oversight—through focusing on systems, personnel, and resources—covers much more territory than does quality assurance.

7. When is oversight not appropriate? How does one decide?

The disastrous examples of IS failures mentioned earlier are evidence of how critical, pervasive, and risk-laden IS activities have become. As a result, oversight of information services activities will *always* be appropriate. Recall the original definition of oversight: maintaining and assuring the existence of effective controls over all IS activity. Oversight is not the hands-on, direct, day-to-day monitoring of IS activities; it is the assurance of an architecture and managerial framework within which these monitoring activities take place.

Rather than asking "how does one decide when oversight is not appropriate?" the question should be "how much and what kind of oversight is appropriate to my situation"? To answer this question, we must first identify the level of risk that senior management is willing to accept. Next we must look at the available risk reduction mechanisms (oversight), and ask: (a) what is the cost of each mechanism? and (b) by how much would our risk exposure decrease if the mechanism were applied? The key to assessing oversight is the use of a cost/benefit framework. It does not make sense to spend more for oversight than the amount that oversight can reduce your risk (potential loss). Of course, this requires that we understand where the risks are. An organization's vulnerabilities are no longer confined to financial systems. Some non-financial systems have the potential to cause serious damage to an organization. Also, timing, resources, and personnel should not be overlooked as risk areas. The potential impact of all these risks must be assessed in order to make a decision about the appropriate level of oversight.

8. How does one guarantee the integrity of the infrastructure in decentralization?

TRANSFORMING THE IS ORGANIZATION

Guaranteeing the integrity of the infrastructure within the context of *any* organizational structure is one role of oversight. The oversight system should assure that the procedures, infrastructure, and managerial structure exist to allow the smooth operation of IS. We need to remember, though, that oversight happens through people. In order to get the full benefit of the oversight procedures, both top management and the user community must agree on the role and importance of oversight.

Oversight activities can be administered in several different ways: (a) through organizational means such as establishing appropriate reporting relationships; (b) by using protective measures such as standards and guidelines; (c) by providing adequate training for all individuals inside and outside IS; (d) through inspections and reviews; and (e) through the use of reports and records. These methods vary in their efficacy based on situational factors such as the cost of the oversight method, the timeliness provided by the method, and the urgency of the information.

9. How do cooperative arrangements with external parties support the core mission of the organization better?

The cooperative arrangements described in Chapter 4 can have a profound effect on an organization's ability to carry out its mission. In most cases, an organization's core mission will be based on such goals as increased productivity, new markets, becoming more competitive, etc. Organizations that are serious about meeting such goals must include IT as a major factor in their overall strategies. More and more, IT will be a critical factor in separating the successful companies from the unsuccessful.

This puts more pressure on already strained IS organizations. As business clamors for new and different applications, the IS organization will require a more diversified knowledge base to keep up with the organization's demands. Unfortunately, paired with the increased demand for more kinds of applications is the decreased supply of IS professionals with skills to generate such applications. The IS organization is bound to reach a limit on the effort it can expend, so tradeoffs between back office, support functions, and strategic applications will have to be made and internal resources reserved for the more specialized or high-value applications. The option of divesting certain IS-related responsibilities through cooperative arrangements will become not only preferable but necessary.

10. Are IS divestment and decentralization the same thing?

No, divestment and decentralization are not the same. The two practices are not implemented for the same reason and they do not produce the same end result. The divestment of back office and support IS functions discussed earlier is offered as a solution to IS organizations constrained in their capabilities to provide these and other services. Essentially, IS is being called upon to take a much more strategic role in organizations, but without the benefit of additional internal resources. The reality of the situation is that (a) turnover rates are as high as 24 percent; (b) IS experience is being invalidated by drastic changes in the industry; and (c) the number of individuals entering the professional IS field is declining. Dwindling IS resources can no longer be stretched to meet all the firm's demands so divestment of the commodity-type function is becoming a technical and economic necessity.

The decision to decentralize the IS functions centers more on organizational and management issues. First, decentralization is viewed as a means of returning control and ownership of data to end users. End users are becoming more technically sophisticated and, as a result, want the power to determine, collect, maintain, and "own" the data they need to do their jobs. Decentralization supports this trend. Second, as information technology drives more of an organization's activities, it is only natural and appropriate that line managers have authority over all the resources that lead to business success. Finally, in an operational sense, decentralization is a strategy that helps ensure a network's viability, that is, the business could still function if one unit on the network went down.

INDEX

A

ABC, 51
Activities matrix, 114
Advisory boards, 48–50, 70
Airline distribution networks, 51
Air Products and Chemicals, 71
Alamo Rent A Car, 79
American Airlines, 46, 91
American Council on Education, 84
American Express, 50
American Hospital Supply, 46
American Industries, 72
Austin Rover Group, 90
Avon, 70

B

Banking industry, 25, 30, 50–51, 94
Bank of New York, 100
British Airlines, 46
British Leyland, 90
British Petroleum, 50, 77
Business platform, 57–58

C

Canadian Institute of Chartered Accountants, 104
Capital investment policies, 76–77
Career ambiguity, 32
Career development. *See also* Education; Human resources management
 avoiding skills erosion, 124
 changing roles, 13–14, 18–25
 lateral, 32–34, 73, 125
 priorities, 28–29
 traditional, 6, 18–19
Chief Information Officer (CIO). *See also* Management role
 oversight responsibility, 101, 104–105, 107, 111, 119–120
 title, 42
CIBA-GEIGY, 77
Cigna Corporation, 72
Citibank, 49–50
Citibank Latino, 46
Citicorp, 60, 71
Communications integration, 18, 20–21, 42
Consultants, 72–73, 91–92

Continental Bank, 64, 75
Control systems
 compared with oversight, 101–102, 105–107, 115
 partnership relations and, 76–79
Cooperative processing, 92
Cooperative relationships. *See* External cooperative relationships
Cycle-sharing, 91

D

Decentralization
 avoiding skills erosion, 124
 compared with divestment, 129
 infrastructure integrity and, 127–128
 market approach view of, 86–87
 oversight and, 106–107
 trends, 1–2, 12–13, 57–59, 67–68, 83–84
 viewed as a technology transfer process, 55–57
Delegation, 48–50
Digital Equipment Corporation, 91
Divestment, 90, 129
Dun and Bradstreet, 51

E

Education. *See also* Career development
 barriers to, 38–39
 case study: Royal Bank of Canada, 36–38
 insularity and, 51–52, 125
 topics, 35
 types of, 34–35
Empire Blue Cross/Blue Shield, 70
External cooperative relationships
 for back office and support applications, 89–92
 guidelines for, 96–97
 mission and, 128–129
 motivations for, 88–89
 overview, 11–12, 83–87
 for strategic applications, 92–96
 types of, 88–89
Exxon Structured Analysis and Design Technique (SADT), 30

F

First Union, 71
Ford, 11–12, 95–96

131

INDEX

Foreign Corrupt Practices Act, 108
Freedom to fail and to succeed, 60–61, 126
Frito-Lay, 72
Full-equity ownership, 88, 90–91, 93–94

G

Geisco, 50, 91
General Electric, 44, 91
GSI, 91, 93

H

Hartford Life, 72
Honeywell, 99
Houston Power & Light, 72
Human resources management. *See also* Career development
  education, 34–39, 51–52, 125
  lateral development, 32–34, 125
  recommendations, 17–18, 39–40
  recruiting, 25–32
Hybridization. *See* Career development

I

IBM, 11–12, 91, 95–96
IBM Canada, 52, 70
Incentive schemes, 78–79, 125–126
Industry Manufacturing Automation Protocol (IMAP), 96
Information Services Activities Matrix, 114
Infrastructure integrity, 3, 127–128
Innovation
  climate for, 60–61, 126
  management role in, 62–65
  recommendations, 79–80
Insularity, 50–52
Internal pricing systems, 77–78
Intra-company relationships
  among managers, 52–54, 61–67, 123–124
  current context, 57–59
  freedom to fail and to succeed, 60–61, 126
  incentive systems for developing, 125–126
  mechanisms of, 65–79
  overview, 10–11, 55–57, 123–124
  recommendations, 79–80
Ireland Industrial Development Authority, 91

J

James A. Cummings Inc., 99

Joint application development (JAD), 52, 70–71, 95–96
Joint ventures
  cooperative, 88, 94–95
  intra-company, 68, 73

L

Lateral development, 32–34, 73, 125. *See also* Career development
Liaison positions, 71–72
Lotus Development Corporation, 91, 99

M

Management role
  agenda for, 41
  authority and responsibility, 42–44
  ending delegation, 48–50
  ending insularity, 50–52, 54
  in innovation, 60–65, 79–80, 126
  mission clarification, 44–48
  mutuality, 52–54
  overview, 7–10
  stereotypical roles, 42–44
Management systems, 73–79
Manufacturers Hanover Trust, 13
Marketing programs, 64–65
Merrill Lynch, 50
Metaphor, 95
Metropolitan Life, 72
Middle management, 64–65, 80. *See also* Management role
Mission
  agenda for accomplishing, 5
  clarifying, 44–48
  cooperative arrangements and, 128–129
  example of mission statement, 3–5
  new, 2–3
  philosophy of partnership, 47
Mobil, 50
Morgan Stanley, 6–7

N

National Institutes of Health, 79
New Jersey Division of Motor Vehicles, 100
New York Life, 70
Norton Company, 64

O

Oversight
  compared with internal control, 101–102

132

INDEX

compared with quality assurance, 126–127
current procedures, 105–107
designing a system for, 107–120
mechanisms for, 114–120
need for, 102–103
overview, 12, 99–101
principles of, 107–111
recommendations, 120–121
responsibility for, 101–102, 103–105, 111
situation-specific, 127
work content view of, 111–112
workflow view of, 112–114
Owens-Corning, 64

P

Partial ownership, 88, 94–95
Partnership mechanisms, 65–67
Partnership relations. *See* Intra-company relationships
Petrochemical industry, 30
Pfizer, Inc., 75
Philosophy of partnership, 47
Planning mechanisms, 74–76
Politics of ambiguity, 7–8, 41, 42–44, 49–50, 54

Q

Quality assurance, 126–127
Questions and answers, 123–129

R

Recruiting, 25–32
Relationship building. *See* External cooperative relationships; Intra-company relationships
Remote computing services (RCS), 92
Retail Automation Project, 93–94
Risk management. *See* Oversight
Roles. *See also* Career development
analysis of, 20–25
categories of, 21–24
overview, 5–7
versus tasks, 19–20
Royal Bank of Canada (RBC)
education programs, 36–38
intra-company relationships, 10–11
liaison positions, 72
mission statement, 3–5, 46

S

Sara Lee Company, 9–10
Sears, 48–49, 50
Security Pacific, 78, 79
Senior management. *See* Management role
Service level agreements, 78
Sheffield, 99–100
Skill base. *See also* Career development
avoiding skills erosion, 124
recommendations, 17–18
role analysis, 20–25
role definition, 19–20
traditional, 18–19
Steering committees, 48–50, 69, 123
Strategic planning, 74
Structural overlays, 68–73
Syntelligence, 93, 96
Systems development, 2
Systems planning, 74

T

Task Forces, 70
Technology planning, 74
Technology platform, 57–58, 112
Technology transfer groups, 71
Technology Ventures, 94
TEKNOWLEDGE, 95
Transaction cost theory, 85–87
Transaction Technology, Inc. (TTI), 71
Transcomm Data Systems (TDS), 93
Travelers Corporation, 62, 91
Triangle Underwriters Inc., 99

U

Union Carbide, 72
University of California at Los Angeles, 84

V

Volvo, 50

W

Wang Corporation, 91

X

Xerox, 71

133

ABOUT THE AUTHORS

Joyce J. Elam is known for her research on the use of information technology to support decision-making activities of both individuals and groups. Her work has appeared in such journals as *Decision Sciences, Decision Support Systems,* and *Interfaces*. Elam is currently an associate professor in the Management Science and Information Systems Department at the University of Texas. During the 1987-88 academic year, she served as the Marvin Bower Fellow at the Harvard Business School. Prior to joining the University of Texas, Elam taught at the Wharton School.

Michael J. Ginzberg has 15 years' experience in the area of implementation and management of information processing technology as a teacher, author, researcher, and consultant. He is currently the chairman of Management Information and Decision Systems at the Weatherhead School of Management, Case Western Reserve University. He previously served on the faculties of Columbia University's Graduate School of Business, New York University's Graduate School of Business Administration, and the Sloan School of Management at MIT.

Peter G.W. Keen is a recognized leader in the information technologies management field and is one of the country's top MIS advisors. In addition to being the executive director of the International Center for Information Technologies, Keen is an established author and educator. He has served on the faculties of the Harvard Business School, Massachusetts Institute of Technology, and Stanford University. He has also taught at the Wharton School of Business and the London Business School.

Robert W. Zmud has conducted extensive research on the impact of information technologies and on organizational efforts in planning and managing information technologies. He is a professor and Thomas L. Williams Jr. Eminent Scholar in the Information and Management Sciences Department at the Florida State University College of Business. He has also authored several books and articles for academics and practitioners in the information technologies field.